Three Wishes

A Mulberry Lane Novel, Volume 2

Melissa Crosby

Published by iHeart Press, 2020.

Copyright

ISBN - 978-0-9951379-3-6
Print ISBN 978-0-9951379-4-3

MULBERRY LANE SERIES – INSPIRATIONAL WOMEN'S FICTION

Read the whole series:

About This Book

They say bad things come in threes.

Welcome back to Mulberry Lane! Two years have passed, and it's time to get reacquainted with best friends, Kate, Sarah, and Louise.

When Kate accidentally breaks a mirror, she believes she's destined for seven years of bad luck. And just as the superstition dictates, a stream of tragedies crops up, beginning with the sudden death of her father.

Sarah and Caleb have good news to share: They are taking their commitment to another level and are moving in together. Everything is perfect until Sarah makes a regrettable mistake that completely over-turns their bliss.

After forty years apart, Louise is finally in the arms of Philip, the man she'd once lost to God. But their happiness is short-lived when Louise receives a life shock that will change everything forever.

Kate, Sarah, and Louise find themselves in the face of misfortune and adversity of which they are powerless to change. Will the bonds of their friendship continue to give them strength? Join them in this story about mothers and daughters, friendship, life, and love.

Three Wishes is an heartfelt and emotional novel about family, relationships, and life in its purest form.

Acknowledgements

To Wayne, my husband, my rock, and my best friend. Thank you for always having my back. In return, I promise to always laugh at your jokes.

To Rev Ben Johnson-Frow. Thank you for taking my numerous phone calls and messages. Whenever I find myself in a bind, I think not only of *What Would Jesus Do*, but also, *What Would Ben Do*?

Until the next book,

Melissa Crosby

Prologue

They say all bad things come in threes.
~Unknown

1 month earlier

Kate Morgan

S*even years*, Kate thought as she got down on her knees. Careful not to cut herself, she picked up the broken mirror pieces and placed them one by one in the empty shoe box she'd found sitting in the garage. "Seven years," she mumbled under her breath.

Everyone knew that a broken mirror was a bad thing. At least every Filipino did.

A broken mirror symbolized one's shattered soul; one that would take years to put back together—seven years, to be exact. And for Kate, having grown up in the Philippines with every superstition ingrained into her psyche, she feared the string of bad luck that lay ahead of her.

She couldn't work out how it happened. One minute, she was gazing proudly at the decorations she'd set up for her son Adam's birthday party that afternoon. And the next minute—she'd heard a loud crash that caused her to jump out of her skin.

The mirror by the front door had fallen off the hook that had held it up for years before she'd even set foot in the United States.

A shiver ran down her spine as she glimpsed herself in some pieces. Three eyes, side by side, stared back at her; the rest of her face split in ten or twenty different ways. Pins and needles ran across her lips.

"Don't worry about it," Sarah said when she and her family arrived. "It's just a mirror."

"I can't!" Kate whispered, as if not wanting the spirits to further her misfortune. Anyone could have easily said she was crazy, maybe even paranoid. She couldn't. Not after the last two years. Those were terrible enough. Another seven would just break her.

"Kate, calm down." Sarah glanced at her boyfriend, Caleb. "Could you take over from Kate, honey?"

"Yeah, of course." Caleb jumped into action. "You guys take the kids to the garden and I'll take care of this." By the kids, Caleb was referring to Sarah's children, Liam, Noah, and Zoe—bless their cute little blonde heads.

"My goodness, what's happened here?"

Kate looked up to see Louise. Standing behind her were her partner Philip and her stepdaughter Abby. "Ugh," Kate groaned. "Seven years of bad luck—that's what."

Philip took a step forward. "I'll help Caleb with this," he said to Louise. "You ladies go relax. Are the others in the garden?" Philip asked Kate, who nodded.

Kate watched Philip—Minister Philip Burns of St. Anthony's Church, the love of Louise's life—crouch next to Caleb, helping him sweep her irrational fears away. It was funny (not funny) how many Filipinos were so fervently religious and yet highly superstitious.

Kate was the complete package. She was part of one-too-many generations who had been raised in fear. There was the fear of the Lord which had been so heavily instilled in her by the nuns who taught her at the private all-girls Catholic school she'd attended from Kindergarten through to College. Then, the fear of the devil—said with a small "d" and not a capital "D", as doing so would only embolden the presence of evil. And lastly, fear of the unknown. Being educated in the private school system taught her that she always needed to have a plan, for a plan provided structure. With that all said, it was no surprise that Kate was a bundle of nerves.

"Come now, darling,"—Louise took Kate by the shoulders and led her out of the way—"where is the birthday boy?"

"With Evan," Kate said. "They went to park, so I could focus on getting ready for the party."

"And Mark?"

Mark was Kate's boyfriend—or friend. Or special friend, maybe. She hadn't really put a label to it yet. In the last two years, they've grown close to each other. Mark helped her to laugh when things were difficult. He showed her that love does not expect. Love does not dictate. And love does not raise a hand to inflict pain. All very different from her experiences being married to her ex-husband, Evan. "He's got a few deliveries to complete today, and then he'll join us as soon as he's done." Being a courier had its demands, and Kate was grateful that he always tried to be available, though it was not always possible. She turned to Louise. "This wasn't supposed to happen."

"I know, dear. But life likes to play games with us, remember?" Louise smiled. Ever-knowing, calm, together...that was Louise, and Kate loved her dearly.

"No—I mean...you don't understand." They were meant to enjoy a lovely high-tea themed birthday party for her son, Adam. It wasn't supposed to happen like this. The mirror wasn't supposed to fall; and she wasn't supposed to glimpse her shattered soul. But then again—she wasn't supposed to be a twenty-seven-year-old divorcee.

Poor Kate's heart slipped right off her sleeve. There was no way she could have predicted the haunting cloud of superstition that hung above her head.

Louise Delaney

AFTER ALL EVIDENCE of Kate's impending seven years of bad luck had been put aside, Louise stood over the birthday boy with a pair of scissors in her hand. "Tell me again, darling,"—she looked at Kate—"why are we cutting Adam's hair?"

Kate stood holding her ex-husband's hair clippers and beamed, "Because he's now two-years-old, and I was supposed to have cut it when he turned one."

"Yes, but why do we need to cut his hair?" Sarah asked, holding yet another pair of scissors. She ran her fingers through Adam's brown wavy hair and glanced at Louise. "He's got such beautiful hair," she said wistfully, and pretended to pout.

"Well, 'cuz that's what Filipinos do. When you shave a baby's hair on their first birthday, it promotes healthy regrowth. Then they have beautiful hair when they're older," Kate said without missing a beat. "But before that, you and Sarah are going to cut off the first locks and then I'm going to keep them between the pages of this book." Kate picked up a book that she had set aside: The Happiness Project. "The belief is that if the first cut is given by someone intelligent, then the child grows up to be intelligent too. You and Sarah are both intelligent women—intellectually and emotionally—so you're the perfect people to give Adam his first cut," she said, as if it was the most normal thing in the world.

"But if he's two now, then doesn't that defeat the purpose?" Sarah asked.

"I still need to do it, so might as well do it now," Kate said.

Louise shook her head and sighed, "Okay—the mama bear has spoken." It was hard to keep up with Kate's beliefs and superstitions, some of which were rather unconventional, even bordering on ridiculous; but Louise loved her friend dearly and respected her culture. Holding up a lock of Adam's hair, Louise brought the scissors close, ready to take the first snip.

"Wait!" Kate blurted. She turned to Evan. "Are you ready?"

Evan held his phone up, poised to take the action photo. "You're sure you wanna do this, right?"

Louise had to give it to Evan. After everything that the couple—now exes—had been through, Evan had pulled his head in and was doing everything he could to be a good father. Looking at the doting dad, no one outside of their circle would ever guess that there was a time when he did not want his son; even going as far as raising his hand and threatening Kate against having him. No one, except the town sheriff, who had arrested him for domestic violence and public intoxication. Despite her meek and nervous nature, Kate firmly stood her ground and vowed to have—and raise—her unexpected blessing; later teaching Evan that nothing could whip a mother's love down. She had to admit; at first, Louise was doubtful that Evan could change. He was an alcoholic and a violent drunk. But he had changed. Every day. One step at a time.

"Evan, yes! We talked about this." Kate stood with a hand on her hip, no longer the shy girl she once was.

"Okay, okay,"—Evan laughed and rubbed his beard—"let's get on with it then."

Louise was pleased for both her friends. Just a couple of years before, life had dealt them each a difficult hand. And just when it seemed they had hit rock bottom, they—Kate, Sarah, and Louise—had found each other. Together, their strength was doubled, even tripled, lifting each other up even when it felt they no longer had the energy or spirit.

When Sarah's husband Adam died unexpectedly, Louise and Kate picked her up and walked every step with her. They did not judge her—not when depression had invaded her life, or when she couldn't care for her children, who were all under the age of five at the time. Not even when she'd fallen for Caleb so soon after Adam's death.

And when Evan kicked Kate out of the house over an unwanted pregnancy, threatening her with violence and deportation, Louise took her into her own home, providing food, shelter, safety, and friendship. Both she and Sarah stayed with her in the delivery room and encouraged her through the pain and triumph of birth. Louise had even endured sleepless nights when the baby was born.

For Louise, it was Kate and Sarah, who had stood by her and lent her their wings when she first found out (sixteen years later) that her very own late husband Warren had fathered another daughter, after they had lost their youngest one to SIDS. There was also that time her first love, Philip, had returned home forty years after serving—first, as a Deacon, then a Priest, and later, a Reverend—telling her that he had always loved her.

Louise smiled at the women around her and marveled at the significant parts they played in each other's lives. Some men came along, and some went; but her friendship with these women—that was there to stay. It was real and tangible, and it would keep growing, keep them whole; and keep them strong.

Sarah Gardner

"COME ONE, YOU GUYS," Sarah said as Adam let out a cry—likely because of growing impatience towards the adults milling around him. "Adam," Sarah sang and smoothed his cheek with her free hand. "Don't cry, honey. Okay,"—she looked up from the birthday boy—"let's do this if we're going to do this. The kids will wreak havoc soon." She looked across the garden where her own children chased after each other. Caleb carried Zoe on his shoulders while Liam and Noah jumped up to reach her.

"No fair," Noah cried, scrunching his little face. "Zoe's too high to catch!"

Sarah smiled. Caleb had been a constant in their lives—a good kind of constant. And their relationship had blossomed into something more than she could have ever hoped for; not after losing her husband—her best friend, her rock. When Adam died, it seemed like he had taken the life out of everything along with him. When Caleb came into her life, it was like a sliver of hope had opened up.

It wasn't easy though. She had to fight the overwhelming feelings of guilt that consumed her. It wasn't normal for a widow to fall so easily for someone else, whatever that means. It wasn't supposed to happen, and people didn't like it. They whispered. They passed rumors around like hot potatoes. Had it not been for Kate and Louise, Sarah could have lost her babies to child services. She might have well lost herself completely.

"Alright, is everyone ready?" Kate called.

"Yes!" Sarah and Louise replied in unison, both poised to take the first snips of Adam's hair.

"Kids,"—Caleb rounded the kids together—"they're starting!"

"On the count of three!" Kate smiled excitedly. "One—two—" But her phone rang. Kate cast a quick glance at it and then looked at Sarah. "It's my mother." Kate felt her stomach turn. Her mother never called.

"What?" Sarah looked up, hand on hip.

Kate put a hand up, ultimately pausing the ceremony. "Hello?"

Adam cried again, more insistent than before.

"Okay, that's enough for now." Evan undid the straps of Adam's chair and picked his restless son up in his arms.

"What?" Kate's voice quivered. She glanced at Sarah and then Louise.

"Is everything okay?" Sarah mouthed.

Kate pulled out a chair and sat down. "When? How?" she spoke into the phone.

Sarah sat down next to her.

"What's going on?" Louise asked.

"I don't know," Sarah whispered. "It's her mom." Sarah knew Kate didn't have a very good relationship with her mother—at least not since Kate had disappointed her by leaving the Philippines to follow Evan to the United States.

Kate bit her bottom lip, and tears flowed from her eyes. "Okay," she whispered into the phone. "I love you too."

"What's happened?" Louise asked when Kate ended the call. "Is everything alright?"

Kate looked up at them; her face drained of any life. "That was my mom."

Sarah took Kate's hand in hers. "What did she say?"

"It's my dad," Kate said. "He's dead."

Summer

It is better to light a candle than curse the darkness.
~Eleanor Roosevelt

Chapter 1

Kate Morgan

Twenty-seven-year-old Kate Morgan was a God-fearing and highly superstitious person who never clipped her nails a night or put her handbag on the floor. She looked away whenever a black cat crossed her path, and she checked the doors and locks three times before bed each night.

Sweet as she was, Kate was always eager to please and had an insatiable need for love and approval, even at the expense of her own happiness. If given the opportunity, it wouldn't have been difficult for a psychologist to determine that she was the way she was due to her upbringing. At the end of the day, we are all products of our relationships and experiences, both past and present. Our parents, siblings. Aunties and uncles. Our babysitters and teachers. Our best friends, the first boys who'd ever broken our hearts—as well as the last ones. The man behind the counter in the corner store who refused to sell us the candy when we were nine-years-old because we were ten cents short; even the recluse across the street. Those are the relationships that have shaped who each of us are today and who we will be tomorrow.

Kate paced the waiting area with Adam in her arms. A mix of anticipation and dread filled her. The airport was just as busy as it had been on the day she'd first flown into Portland on her way to Carlton Bay. Evan had been there, waiting for her, flowers in one hand and balloons in the other. She remembered the giddiness she'd felt when she spotted him. It was the first day of the rest of her life; her new life, which belied how that marriage would later end

"Babe, stop pacing," Mark said. "Everything's gonna be fine."

Kate was relieved that Mark was able to get the afternoon off from work so that he could help her pick her mother up from the airport. "I'm so excited!" Kate was very close to her mom. She was her best friend and the one person—apart from Adam and her best friends, Sarah and Louise—who she loved most in the word. But she was also nervous. Ever since the day she'd told her parents she was leaving for the United States to be with Evan, her mother had all but disowned her. "But I'm also scared." Kate dry-retched. "I think I'm gonna be sick. What time is it?" Kate checked her watch. It was almost 1:00pm. Her mom's flight should have arrived at 12.20pm from Manila and the flight board said it had landed on time.

"She should be coming out of the customs area any minute now." Mark took Adam from Kate. "But seriously, babe, you've gotta relax. You're making me nervous!"

"Don't be nervous. My mom is super cool," Kate said, as if also trying to convince herself.

"You told her I'd be here, right?" Mark asked.

Kate and Mark had been dating for close to two years now. They'd decided to take things slow. Or—more accurately—she'd decided to take things slow. After her one-year marriage to Evan ended up in divorce, the last thing she wanted was to get tied up in another relationship. The next stage in her life was dedicated to finding out who she was as an adult, an independent woman, and a new mother. "Of course," Kate beamed and then scrunched her face. "I mean, I didn't exactly tell her you'd be here; like, today. But I have told her all about you and how amazing you are," she quickly added.

"What? You mean she doesn't know I'm out here waiting with you?" Mark asked.

Kate shrugged. "Don't worry. She's cool—and you're gonna love her." For what it was worth, Helen Valdez was a great mom. She was a great woman, the kind of person who didn't take fools. She called things as she saw them.

Growing up, Kate watched in awe how Helen carried herself. To Helen, a spade was a spade—there were no two ways about it. And if anyone tried to sell her a shovel, claiming it to be a spade, that person was in for it. There was black, there was white, but there was never gray. Helen was fierce and beautiful, and she was wise. Everyone loved her. "Do you know...when I was younger, my mom taught PE at my school. She would wear these colorful leotards and tights—like the one's Jane Fonda used to wear in the eighties," Kate laughed. "I wasn't in her class, of course, though I wish I had been. All the students thought she was cool, and I was super proud she was my mom. Anyway, when the nuns found out that she was wearing those outfits and teaching her students aerobics, they told her she needed to stop. Right? I mean, it was a strict private Catholic school for girls. They'd expected her to get the kids to do jumping jacks, sit-ups, and push-ups."

Mark nodded as he listened to Kate's story.

"But my mom wasn't having any of it. She always made things fun. So, for her next class, she got her students to come in the most colorful aerobics outfits they could find; and for PE, they jogged around the school campus with two of her students carrying a boombox, blasting Billy Joel's Uptown Girl on the loudest volume setting." Kate laughed at the memory of it. "It was so funny! I was so proud to be her daughter."

"Then what happened?"

"She quit."

"She quit her job?" Mark asked.

"Yup! Right on the spot and guess what her exit music was?"

Mark wrinkled his handsome nose. "She marched off to an exit song?"

"She danced away to that song by James Brown—I Feel Good."

"Do I know the song?"

"Everybody knows the song," Kate said. "I feel good,"—she sang— "na na na na na na na—that's the guitar!" she laughed. "I knew that I would now, na na na na na na na."

"Oh, I know that one"—he sang along—"so good! And it's a saxophone, not a guitar," Mark laughed. "Might even be a trumpet."

"So good!" Kate echoed him. "I got you!" Kate danced and nuzzled Adam's neck, sending him into a fit of giggles.

"She sounds like a real treat," Mark said of Helen.

"Oh, she is! Mom was always the life of the party. Like, seriously, she could walk into a wake and the whole sad affair would turn into a party." Kate was beginning to look forward to seeing her mom walk through the gates.

"Come here, buddy," Mark said as he picked Adam up from Kate's arms.

"You know... when I broke that mirror last month, I thought it was the end. I mean, seven years of bad luck, Mark. First, my dad died. Then, I couldn't afford to fly home to say goodbye. But now," Kate smiled, "now, my mom's coming to live with me. It feels like things are actually falling in place."

Mark laughed. "I think we all knew you were being silly about the whole thing. First of all, you didn't break the mirror. It fell. Whatever bad luck you think comes with that should not fall on you. Second, it was impractical to return to the Philippines. It's not your fault that you weren't able to attend his funeral."

"Whatever," Kate waved a hand in front of her. "I'm just glad. My luck is turning; I can feel it!"

"Kate! Kate!"

Kate saw her mother, Helen, waving from across the way. She wore a deep red dress which fell just above the knees. "Ma!" Kate jumped and waved. She took Adam back from Mark. "There she is," she exclaimed, any of her earlier worries dissipated. "Let's go!"

"My goodness! You've put on so much weight—I almost didn't recognize you," Helen said, laughing. "What have you been eating?"

"It's the baby weight," Kate smiled. "How was the flight?" She noticed her mother wasn't wearing a bra. "Oh my golly gosh, are you not wearing a bra?" Kate whispered and looked around. Helen roared with laughed and cupped her breasts. "I took them off in the flight. You know how I hate bras. My boobs were suffocating. And besides, these babies are so small, no one can even tell they're dancing freely. I'm surprised you can tell." Another roar followed. "Oh, I definitely felt it." Kate laughed. Helen always brought the entertainment and wasn't afraid to laugh at herself.

"Anyway, I'm glad you're here. Woohoo!" She was a blast of energy.

"That bad?" Kate asked.

"I was worried about having to wait around another minute," Helen said. "Standing around in the customs area is such a waste of time. They asked me so many questions—you'd think I was a terrorist or something."

"Sssh...Ma! Don't say that," Kate said in a hushed tone and looked around to see if anyone had heard her.

Helen instantaneously frowned. "And why not? I can say whatever I want to say, thank you very much!"

The sudden shift in Helen's tone surprised Kate. "I know you can...but still."

"I can and I did," Helen said with an air of nonchalance. "So there!" She looked Mark up and down.

Mark grinned. "Hello, Mrs.—"

"Oh good, here,"—Helen handed Mark her hand carry bags—"you can take these for me. Now, where is my little grand-son," she said, turning back to Kate and focusing on Adam. "Come to Mama Helen, you handsome little baby," she cooed.

"No, Ma, wait, this is Mark..." A nervous laugh escaped from her mouth. Whilst she was eager for her mother to bond with her Adam, she didn't want Helen to think that Mark was some a baggage handler. Helen's eagerness at seeing Adam had actually surprised her. Not once had her mother shown any delight—curiosity, tenderness, longing—for her grandson. Helen was one of those for whom the saying 'out of sight, out of mind' held true. But Kate knew that once her mother had met Adam, the relationship would grow.

"Oh," Helen stopped and shook her head. "Sorry—am I supposed to tip him now?" she muttered as she rummaged through her handbag. "My goodness, Kate, why didn't you tell me? I don't think I have any dollars—"

"No, no," Kate sighed. "This is Mark—I told you about him. Remember? Mark is my partner."

"It's nice to meet you, ma'am," Mark tried once more.

"Your partner?" Helen pursed her lips and regarded him, before turning back to Kate. "Where is Evan?"

Kate glanced at Mark and put a hand on his arm as if to reassure him. "I'm sorry," she said to him. Turning back to Helen, "Ma, I told you that Evan and I have gotten a divorce."

Helen looked from Kate to Mark and back at Kate. "Nonsense. I already told you, Filipinos do not get divorced. Now, let me say hello to my grandson please." With a swift move, Helen took Adam from Kate's arms, exchanging her Louis Vuitton handbag for the baby. "How's my handsome grandson? You look just like your father," she cooed. "No, actually, just like your grandfather," she said with an emphasis on the word grand.

Adam cried and wriggled in his grandmother's arms as he reached for Kate.

Helen did not hide her disappointment. "You clearly have never told him about me," she said, handing Adam back to Kate.

Kate sighed. Things were not going as well as she'd hoped. "Ma, he's two-years-old. He'll come around soon. You just need to give him some time."

Helen sniffed. "I suppose we should go. I'm exhausted from the travel." Helen looked at Mark. "Can you at least help me with my luggage?"

Mark nodded. "If you come with me to baggage carousel, you can point yours out and I'll go and grab it."

THINGS DID NOT GET any better during the drive back to Carlton Bay. Helen insisted on bringing up Kate's marriage to Evan. "Can we please talk about this later?" Kate asked, concerned about how Mark would have been feeling.

"You have made a sacred vow, Kate. A vow to your husband and a vow to the Lord. You don't get to just wake up and decide you're over it," Helen persisted.

"I did not just wake up and decide I was over it." Kate stared out the window, longing to be back in her house.

"Kate, *ang pag-aasawa ay hindi biro. Di tulad ng kanin na iluluwa lang pag napaso,*" Helen quoted a Filipino proverb.

Marriage is not a joke; it's not like rice that you can just spit out when it's too hot. Kate had heard it enough times growing up. She was educated in a Catholic school and was taught all about the vows of chastity and marriage, with many hours spent in school sat cross-legged on the floor watching horrifying videos of childbirth designed to encourage celibacy. "I know, Ma."

"Do you really?" Helen pushed, forcing the subject. "Do you think there weren't times when I'd wanted to leave your father? *Aba!*" she exclaimed in Filipino in a bid to drive a point. "But I made a vow, and I upheld that vow until his dying day.

Kate let out a deep sigh as her frustration rose. Feeling Mark take her hand, she glanced at him. "I'm sorry", she whispered. Mark responded with the squeeze of a hand, but kept his eyes on the road.

"And what about Adam?" Helen continued. "Is he going to grow up without his father? Do you have any idea what happens to kids who grow up in broken families? This is not a joke, Katherine Ann!"

Kate only ever heard her full name when she was being scolded. Now twenty-seven-years-old, nothing had changed. "Ma, can we just stop? Please? Evan and I are co-parenting and it's working fine. You're being rude to Mark."

"Co-parenting? What even is that?" Helen spat. "And me? Rude? Well, excuse me! You didn't think it was rude to bring your lover to pick me up? That is no way to greet your mother. And so soon after your father had died! Lord have mercy on us, Katherine Ann—we raised you better than this."

Kate massaged her temples. Her head was throbbing. How did she ever think this was going to be a good idea? She'd romanticized it, thinking they could go back to the days when they were best friends. She was wrong.

Chapter 2

Sarah Gardner

"What do you think?" Sarah asked Louise, her hands resting on her hips. Sarah had offered to host a welcome dinner for Kate's mom. After everything that Kate had been through, she was glad that her friend had something to look forward to.

"Everything looks great," Louise eyed the buffet that Sarah had carefully organized.

"What if she doesn't like this type of food?" Sarah wrinkled her nose.

"Trust me," Louise said, "you've left nothing more to want for—not with this amazing spread. I mean, just look at all that!"

"True," Sarah said, taking another look at the buffet. They had all pitched in. There was a classic garden salad of tomatoes, cucumbers, carrots, feta, and Sarah's now-famous croutons and homemade dressing. Louise had prepared a dish of tender beef tips braised with wine, garden herbs, mushrooms, onion, and potatoes. Caleb threw together a chicken with mustard sauce. And Philip, ever the dessert man, had prepared an Oreo Cheesecake as requested by Sarah's son, Liam. Even Abby—Louise's eighteen-year-old stepdaughter—had baked some chocolate chip cookies. "It's just that Kate has been so looking forward to her mother coming over…I just want everything to be perfect."

"And it is," Louise said in her ever-calming way.

"She sounds like a real hoot, doesn't she?"

Louise made a face. "Who?"

"Kate's mom, I mean."

"Kate's mom?" Louise laughed. "Yes, of course, Kate's mom. Going by all the stories we've heard about her; I know we're all going to get along."

"And it will be really nice for Kate to have some family around, don't you think?" Not that Sarah had any family herself, but it was different for Kate. She hadn't grown up in the Carlton Bay—or in the country, for that matter. And there weren't many Filipinos in the bay area, if any at all.

"Mm-yes, I agree." Louise nodded, her eyes darting around. "I think you and I deserve a cup of tea before they arrive, don't you?" Louise grinned.

"I could certainly use one," Sarah agreed. "I'll put the kettle on."

"I'll get the mugs," Louise said. "Philip? Caleb?" she called out towards the garden where they were hanging out with the children. "Would you gentlemen like some tea?" And when they declined the offer, she reached for two mugs from the cupboard. The three of them—Sarah, Louise, and Kate—all knew each other's homes as if each were their own, spending as much time as they could together in between work, life, and everything else.

Sarah pulled out a box of tea. "English breakfast okay with you?"

Louise nodded. "How are things with you and Caleb?" she asked.

Sarah looked up at Louise and smiled. She had some news to share, but they were planning on telling everyone when they were all together. But Louise asking made it harder to keep it a secret. "Don't tell anyone,"—she said in a hushed tone even if there wasn't anyone around—"we're going to share some news with y'all this evening."

"Ooh," Louise teased. "I like surprises. What is it?"

"Well, if I told you, then it wouldn't be a surprise." Sarah laughed. She took the kettle and poured the hot water into the two mugs.

"My goodness—don't tell me you're pregnant?" Louise asked.

Sarah's eyes widened. "What? No! I don't think I can handle another child at this time," she laughed, shaking her head. "Can you imagine?" Having another child was not on her agenda—not at all.

"No," Louise laughed along. "You had me worried there for a while. Although," she mused, "I wouldn't mind having another baby to cuddle."

"Well then, you go on ahead and make your own baby to cuddle—I'm done," she joked. Sarah loved her kids, but three was all she could handle. After battling with depression, she was becoming more aware of taking time for herself and practicing self-care. She had a long way to go, but every day was another day of triumph.

"That would be a laugh, wouldn't it?" Louise took the mug of tea that Sarah handed to her. "Philip and I with a baby,"

Louise snickered at the thought. "I think we're happy with all the kids between you and Kate. It's like we have instant grandchildren."

Sarah paused and smiled at Louise. "That's so sweet. Do you really think of the kids as your grandkids?" With both her adoptive parents and her late husband's parents gone, the kids had no one to call grandma and grandpa. Sarah blew on her tea and took a cautious sip.

"Of course. I'm too old to be an aunty to the little ones. And besides, grandparents get to do all the spoiling without having to deal with any of the consequences."

Sarah placed a hand over her chest and smiled, furrowing her brows. "You're gonna make me cry."

"Well, don't." Louise waved a hand before her. "And besides, Kate already makes Adam call me Lola, which apparently means grandmother in her language."

"Oh, yes, I've heard her call you that. I think it's so cute. Lola," she let the word roll off her tongue.

"I think it is."

"What does Adam call Philip?" Sarah asked.

"Lolo Philip," Louise grinned.

Sarah laughed. "Aww... Lola and Lolo, that's so sweet," she mused. "Are you okay with being called Lola?"

Louise shrugged. "It's fine by me as long as I get time to spend with them. And it's a nice feeling...being someone's grandmother."

"I should get my kids to call you Lola too. Can I?" Sarah liked the idea. It had a special ring to it. "Lola Louise and Lolo Philip," she said, trying it out once more.

"Oh, I would love that." Louise beamed.

Sarah suddenly caught herself. She hoped their conversation did not trigger anything for Louise. Louise's daughter, Madison, had recently given birth to a daughter and given their long-term estrangement, Louise had only found out through Facebook. "I hope I didn't put my foot in it?"

Louise looked surprised. "What do you mean?"

"I mean...the whole grandmother thing. I should have been more considerate. With everything that's going on between you and Madison, the baby, and—"

Louise sighed. "I've made my bed and now I need to lie in it," Louise said.

"But—"

"It's Madison's choice. She's the mother and she can decide who she lets into her daughter's life."

Sarah nodded.

"Okay, you've asked, and I've answered," Louise said. "Now it's your turn. Tell me what this whole secret thing is."

Sarah let out an unexpected laugh. "You're sly!"

"Oh, I am—go on." Louise rested her chin on her palm and gestured in Sarah's direction. "I'm waiting."

Sarah undid her apron and hung it on the hook on the wall. "Last week, Caleb and I were..." Sarah paused. "You know..."

"No, I don't." Louise was good at getting people to talk. Oh, she was good. "Keep talking."

"Well,"—Sarah sat down next to her—"I'd just put the kids to bed and Caleb had just finished tidying up the kitchen. He'd prepared a cup of tea for me because he knows I like to have tea at night."

"Goodness," Louise exclaimed. "Are you going to tell me or what? Stop with the novel and get straight to the point."

Sarah laughed aloud, but then she couldn't stop and doubled over before she could even begin.

"He made you a cup of tea—and then what?"

Sarah lapsed into a fit of giggles. When she finally regained control and caught her breath, Sarah continued. "I thought it was so sweet of him, you know...there he was waiting for me with a cup of tea. I couldn't help it." Sarah could feel the heat rising in her cheeks. "So I went up and sat on him."

"You sat on him?" Louise made a face. "What do you mean you sat on him?"

"Okay, so you might say I straddled him."

"Oooh-lala...did you run your hands all through his hair?"

"Mm-hmm," Sarah nodded.

"And kissed him slowly?"

"Mm-hmm," Sarah smiled.

"Just say you were seducing him." Sometimes Louise was a bit matter-of-fact.

Sarah laughed again, and even accidentally let out a snort. "Okay, okay. I was seducing him—I don't like that word," she said. "Let's say, I was charming him. He had his hands around the small of my back and his head was tilted backwards. You know what I mean? Like—" Sarah threw her head back for effect. "But I felt myself slipping so I put my feet up on the spindles and—"

"Wait! What's a spindle?"

Sarah pointed to the horizontal bars connected to each of the four legs of the chair she sat on.

"Oh, I see. I didn't know they were called spindles. Okay, go on," Louise said.

"Right," Sarah smiled widely, "so I put my feet on the spindles to sort of push myself up but I must have pushed too hard because they broke off and I put my arms around his neck for balance and Caleb must have felt it too because he grabbed my butt. Naturally, I screamed, and we both fell backwards. I was mortified!"

By that time Louise was laughing hysterically. "I thought you were trying to seduce him, not kill him!"

Sarah could hardly catch her breath. She continued with the story. "And then he goes, 'I think I broke my back,' and of course I panic. I asked him if he really did and he said no. I rolled off his chest and there we were, lying side by side on the kitchen floor."

Louise dabbed at her eyes, still laughing.

"And then he put his arm under my neck and pulled me toward him, and he said, 'we both have been given this second chance, let's take it for what it is.' And there I was, as dense as a brick; I had no idea what he was getting at. Then he said that we should move in together." She'd been smiling from ear to ear over the last few days, just waiting to share the news with Louise and Kate.

"Well, it's about time," Louise said. "He's always here, I'm surprised you guys haven't moved in a lot sooner."

Sarah scrunched her face. "Yeah, but I guess it's different now. Now we both know what we really want."

"Good for you," Louise said. "I'm happy for you both."

"Don't tell the others okay?" Sarah reminded. "We're going to share the news later on tonight."

Louise pretended to zip her lips.

"Hello?"

"They're here!" Sarah beamed excitedly as she got up from her seat. "In the kitchen," she called out, quickly putting aside anything that she saw was out of place.

"Where's the broken chair?" Louise asked.

"What?"

"The broken chair—the one with snapped spindles."

"Oh,"—Sarah grinned—"it's in the garage."

"Hi everyone," Kate walked into the kitchen followed by a much shorter woman, a couple of feet shy of Kate's. Unlike Kate, her mother was tiny—on the verge of skinny—and she did not look at all like the fifty years that Kate said she was. She was hot. "Guys, this is my mom." Kate turned to her mom, "Ma, these are my best friends, Sarah and Louise."

"Mom has a name," Kate's mother said, her smile tight.

"Of course she does," Louise held her arms out and walked towards her. "You must be Helen," she said, taking Kate's mom into an embrace. "I'm Louise,"—she said and then turning to Sarah—"and this is Sarah."

Sarah followed suit and gave Helen a welcome hug. "It's so nice to meet you, Helen." She could sense, having gotten to know Kate very well, that her friend was uneasy. There was something amiss. "Let's go out to the backyard, so you can meet everyone else."

"Oh, there's more?" Helen quipped. It hadn't even been a minute, but already, something about the woman rubbed Sarah the wrong way.

"Ma,"—Kate pleaded—"these are my friends."

"The same ones who'd encouraged you to break your vows, I assume?" Helen didn't hold back. "I am tired, Katherine. It's been a long flight and I'm not in the mood for socializing."

It was hard for Sarah to pretend she didn't hear what the woman was saying. "Let's get you off your feet, Helen."

"I see they have no respect for their elders either," Helen muttered to Kate. "Yes, that would be nice," she said in response to Sarah's offer and followed her through the door, out to the backyard.

"Everyone," Sarah called out, gathering them around Helen. "Kids, everyone—come and meet Kate's mom, Helen." Sarah glanced at Helen and smiled. She hoped that the children would behave. Helen didn't seem like the type who would suffer the antics of children. "Noah!" she called to her middle child who, as usual, had ignored her.

"Helen,"—Philip extended a hand—"I'm Philip Burns. Welcome to Carlton Bay. How was your flight?"

Unlike the smile shared with Sarah and Louise, Helen smiled warmly at Philip and took his hand. "Well, it was a long flight, but I'm glad to be here now."

"Philip is my partner," Louise said, hooking her arm through Philip's. "And I'm Louise."

"Yes, I know—we met just before. How nice for you." Sarah noted the sarcasm in Helen's tone. "And who is this?" she motioned to Caleb.

"I'm Caleb—it's nice to meet you, ma'am." Caleb said politely.

"Oh, please," Helen chuckled once more. "I'm not much older than you. You can call me Helen," she said, holding on to his hand just a tad longer than Sarah was comfortable with.

"Caleb is my partner," Sarah interjected.

It was unexpected. Sarah didn't like the feelings brewing inside her. There was something about Helen—she just couldn't put a finger on it.

Chapter 3

Louise Delaney

Before they all sat down to eat, Louise noticed that Kate and Mark disappeared back into the house; and when Kate returned, she was on her own. "Where's Mark?" she asked.

Kate glanced around the table and then at her mom. "Uhm—he had to go do something for work. Shall we eat?"

It did not escape Louise that Helen had raised an eyebrow as she took a sip from her glass of soda. Louise frowned. "I thought he had the rest of the day off?"

Kate pressed her lips together and shook her head. "He did, but something came up."

"Right, well, we'll catch up with him in the next few days, I'm sure." Louise knew her friend, and she could tell that Kate was hiding something. "So, Heather—Kate tells us that you'll be staying in Carlton Bay for a while."

"It's Helen," Kate's mom corrected her.

"Hmm?"

"My name's Helen, not Heather."

"Goodness! I don't know where my head is at today." Louise felt her cheeks flush. "My apologies," she laughed; a hand on her chest. "I'm not sure where I got Heather from. Have you been to the United States before?" she asked, quickly changing the subject.

Unsmiling, Helen nodded. "Yes, I have some family in California and New York. But it's been a while."

"It must be good to be with family right now. I mean, here, with Kate. I was so sorry to learn of your husband's passing." Whilst she didn't want to bring up the death of Kate's father, Louise thought it best to raise the subject rather than to skirt around it. After all, it was the reason that Helen was in Carlton Bay.

"Thank you, Louise. It was difficult to say goodbye. But that's life, isn't it?" Helen dabbed her eyes with a napkin.

Louise reached across and placed a hand over Helen's. "I'm sorry to have brought it up, darling. It was insensitive of me."

"Oh, not at all," Helen brushed off the apology. "I do get sad when I think about it; but we had twenty-eight years together, and that alone is something to celebrate." Helen raised her glass and nodded. "Cheers."

"It is," Louise sympathized and clinked her glass against Helen's. "I know how it is. My husband, Warren, died a few years ago, and not a day goes by that don't think about him," she said, even if she wasn't being entirely truthful. Just two years ago, she'd learned about Warren's indiscretions when his then sixteen-year-old daughter turned up at her doorstep. It had been a massive blow to her and it took a long time to learn to accept it and move on; to forgive—though not necessarily to forget.

In the last couple of years, Louise had bonded with her stepdaughter, Abby. It had been an unusual situation—having taken Abby in, treating the girl as her own daughter, and building a strong relationship with her. But at the end of day, Louise was grateful for the girl and it honored her to be her stepmom.

"Oh? So, Philip is not your husband?" Helen asked.

"Ma..." Kate warned.

"No, Kate, it's fine. I don't mind," Louise said, assuring her friend. "Philip and I have a long history together," Louise turned to him and smiled, "don't we, darling?" Philip was the love of her life. The one who got away, but eventually returned.

"We sure do." Philip grinned. "Louise and I met when we were just teenagers."

Louise studied his face. He was such a handsome man. Pushing sixty-five, he still took her breath away.

"Really?" Helen clicked her tongue. "That's really quite special, isn't it? My husband and I got married when we were just nineteen."

"I probably would have married Philip, had he not run away to marry God," Louise laughed. It had always been a sore spot for her, but since his return, the hurt had slowly faded. There was once upon a time when she was resentful of him and how he'd chosen God over her.

Helen looked surprised. "Are you a priest?"

"Yes, ma'am, I am." Philip nodded in that priestly way. Louise wondered what Philip would look like if he weren't a priest. She found him both manly and commanding of respect in a way that wasn't arrogant. Truth be told, Louise thought Philip was the sexiest man alive.

"And you can be in a relationship?" Helen asked, shock painted across her face.

"I don't think I could restrain myself if he wasn't allowed to be my man," Louise joked. "If you know what I mean," Louise added, throwing a little tiger growl at Philip, and then burst out with laughter.

"What does it mean, anyway—this whole partner thing? He's her partner,"—she said motioning to Caleb and Sarah—"and you two are partners."

"Well, it means that we're in a relationship with each other. A committed relationship." Louise felt herself glow. She was proud to have Philip as her man. He made her feel giddy, and she enjoyed being in love again.

"So, you have sex?" Helen asked.

"Oh my gosh, Ma!" Kate blushed.

"What?" Helen looked at her daughter. "You sound like a cow—Maaaaaa! Maaaaa!" she said. "Or is it a goat?"

A moment of shock passed through the table before they all erupted in laughter. "Well, I would hope so," Louise threw her head back. She was going to be sixty-one in December and had little time for niceties and holding her feelings back. She'd earned the right to talk about anything and everything she wanted to talk about.

"But he's a priest." Helen appeared unimpressed. "Where I come from, priests aren't allowed to marry or be in relationships."

"Well, thank goodness I'm not from there," Louise joked, causing another eruption of laugher across the table.

"Don't priests take a vow of celibacy?"

"I'm an Anglican priest," Philip explained. "The church does not impose restrictions on marriage. There was once a time when it wasn't allowed, but that was a very long time ago." Philip was always so nice; always explaining things. He had such patience that Louise knew she didn't deserve.

"It certainly confused me," Louise said. "When he left for his religious studies, I thought it was the end of the road for us. So I married his best friend." Louise laughed even louder than she did before, grasping Philip's hand.

"And what about her—your daughter?" Helen nodded to the end of the table at Abby.

Kate placed a hand on Helen's arm. "Ma, I really don't think you should—"

"I'd appreciate it, Katherine Ann, if you would stop telling me what I can and cannot say," Helen snapped. She shook her head and turned back to Louise. "I believe my daughter is afraid I'm going to embarrass her." Helen pressed her lips into a tight line.

The sharp exchange between mother and daughter surprised Louise. "Abby is my stepdaughter."

"But I thought you married your husband when you were quite young. Abby, how old are you, dear?"

Abby sat upright at the mention of her name. She glanced at Louise before replying, "I'm eighteen."

Helen pursed her lips. "I see. And she's your stepdaughter, you said?"

Louise could see where Helen was going with her line of questioning. She could practically see the calculations forming in the woman's head. "My husband had an affair. It was after we'd lost our youngest daughter." Louise shifted in her seat but quickly recovered when she felt Philip's hand on the small of her back. "She died of SIDS."

"I think now's a good time for dessert," Sarah piped up; bless her. "Who wants dessert?" she asked, glancing towards Louise.

Louise smiled at Sarah. They all knew each other so well. She was grateful for such wonderful friends. "I would love some," she said.

"I want dessert! I want dessert!" Noah shouted at the top of his six-year-old lungs.

"Noah, what did we say about shouting?" Sarah warned. Noah had just started big school last fall and had been having trouble adjusting. They'd all been helping Sarah with showing him how to slow down and not be so...excitable. But telling a six-year-old to calm down wasn't as easy as one might have hoped.

"You always want dessert," the older boy, Liam, retorted.

"I don't think he needs any more sugar," Helen muttered.

Kate glared at her mother, "Please stop," she muttered. Kate got up from the table. "I'll come and help you," she said to Sarah.

"He's just excited," Louise said. She was fully aware of how Sarah felt about Noah's big personality—particularly around new people—and she didn't want Helen's comment to add fuel to Sarah's insecurities about her middle child. "That's our Noah," she said, "and we wouldn't have him any other way."

"Would you like some too, Zoe?" Sarah asked her youngest child.

Zoe smiled and nodded. "Yes, please, Mommy." Contrary to her older brother, at just four-years-old, Zoe had beautiful manners.

Chapter 4

Kate Morgan

Kate followed Sarah into the kitchen. It made little sense. Nothing was going right. She couldn't comprehend what was happening or why her mother was being so—so...she couldn't even find the words for it. This was not her mother. Sure, they'd had their differences in the past. Every mother and daughter did. Every relationship did. But this was her mother—they were tight, they were best friends. Kate thought that with Helen choosing to come and live with her, any disappointment she'd had caused her parents by following Evan to the United States had been forgiven. It was clear that this was not the case at all.

When Kate first told her parents that she was moving to the United States to be with Evan, her mother was the first to voice her displeasure and disappointment. *"Ang kita sa bula, sa bula rin mawawala,"* Helen had warned her.

Kate had scoffed. "What comes from bubbles will disappear with bubbles? That doesn't even make any sense!" She'd never been belligerent, but love made her feel like a queen—she was on top of the world and nothing could bring her down, not even her mother's words of wisdom or, on the polar opposite of that scale, her snide and cutting remarks.

"You think that champagne and strawberries mean love? You've only known him for a minute, Katherine. Don't be so stupid!"

Kate had winced when her mother called her stupid. She wasn't being stupid. She was doing what anyone in love would do. She was following her heart, heeding her call—listening to the voice of the universe.

"Are you okay?" Sarah's voice broke through her thoughts.

Kate sighed and bit her lip. "Does it show?" she asked, one eyebrow raised.

Sarah smiled softly—knowingly—and nodded.

"I'm sorry. She's not usually like this." Helen was easy-going and full of life. Everyone loved her. This woman was not the Helen that she knew. It embarrassed Kate that her friends were seeing this side of her mother.

"The trip must have tired her out. Fourteen hours is a long time for anyone. And she'd just lost her husband. You remember how I was when Adam died, right?" It was nice of Sarah to make excuses for her mother. But that's all they were—excuses. As unfortunate as it was, Adam's death was what had brought the three friends together. Kate had only been in the States for about six months then. She'd been incredibly lonely. As it had turned out, her mother was right...the buzz of the champagne had faded and the strawberries had grown rotten. She'd found herself alone in a country where she knew no one. Sarah and Louise had become her best friends, her lifelines. And it was because of their friendship that Kate had named her own son,

Adam, after Sarah's husband. Kate looked at her friend. "Thank you," she said.

"Whatever for?"

"For making excuses." Kate smiled.

"Come here." Sarah pulled Kate into a hug. "It'll be better in the morning—or once the jet lag has worn off," she said with a soft laugh.

"I hope so."

"Me too...she's a bit of porcupine," Sarah said, grinning.

Kate laughed. "I think we both know there are other words that would better suit."

"Apparently, porcupines use their quills to defend against predators," Sarah said. "Noah learned that in school recently—bless him. He won't stop talking about them. So maybe your mom is feeling somewhat out of her element, so she's a bit prickly."

"I thought I would find you two here." Louise appeared at the kitchen backdoor. She took a step in but somehow had tripped and fallen over.

"Oh, my goodness—Louise!" Kate ran to her side. "Are you okay?" she asked as she helped her up.

Louise dusted her knees and fixed her hair. "I'm fine," she said, raising a hand. "I just lost my balance for a moment."

"That's the third time you've fallen this month, Louise," Sarah noted, a worried frown formed across her face.

"I'm fine, I'm fine. I took a wrong step. The floor just seems a tad further as you get older," Louise joked. "Now...what was it I was going to say?" she tapped her lips in thought. After a moment, she said, "It mustn't have been important. The thought has completely slipped away."

"It'll come back to you," Kate said. "How's it going out there? I'm sorry about my mom."

"Sorry? Why?" Louise seemed surprised.

"Her questions...they were a bit personal." Kate crossed her arms over her chest.

"Oh, well," Louise dismissed Kate's concerns with a wave of a hand. "Darling, you needn't worry about that. I've got nothing to hide," Louise said. "I'm an open book. To be honest, I thought it was rather fun going back down memory lane."

Among the three of them, Louise was the wisest. At sixty going on sixty-one, there were few things that Louise let bother her. Over the last few years, it was her wisdom that had helped Kate get through what was the toughest time of her life. And dared she say it, Louise was a like a mother to her.

"And besides, I think it's great that Harriette's asking questions. That means that—"

"It's Helen," Sarah interjected.

Louise paused and looked at her. "What's that, darling?"

"You said Harriette. Kate's mom is Helen."

Louise sighed and tapped two fingers between her eyebrows. "Helen! Why do I keep getting it wrong? Helen, Helen, Helen," she repeated. "Anyway, as I was saying, I'm glad she's asking questions. It's a good way to get all that unease out of the way. Life is too short to walk on eggshells, I say. She's been through a lot. Change is hard. And trust me, change is much more difficult on us older folk."

"I guess..." Kate said tentatively. "I mean, I haven't lived with my parents in a long time. I left home when I started working in another city. But she's not normally like this. She's clearly still mad at me for marrying Evan."

"Let it go. What is normal anyway?" Louise brought her knee up and rubbed it. "Tsk! That smarts."

"Do you want me to get you some ice?" Sarah offered.

"No, no, darling, thanks. I'll be alright."

"Everything okay in here?" Caleb poked his head in from the backdoor. "It's getting a bit awkward without you girls there."

Kate turned around. "Yes, sorry. We're coming," she said. She looked at Sarah. "I guess we should get back out there."

Sarah picked up the Oreo cheesecake that Philip had prepared and handed it to Kate to bring out. "I'll take the cookies Abby made."

Chapter 5

Abby Delaney

Abby Delaney wasn't like most teenagers. As it was, she'd already experienced a lot more than most kids her age. Abby was only sixteen when she ran away from home. She'd left her mom and made the bold move of seeking her stepmother—the one who never knew she existed until that day that Abby turned up at her front porch.

With the help of Louise, Kate, and Sarah, it was fair to say that Abby had turned her life around. She could have easily become a statistic; a child on the streets of Portland. But she didn't. She had Louise to thank for it; but mostly, it was Kate that was really able to get through to her. It may have been because they were closer in age. At the time, Abby was sixteen and Kate was twenty-five.

Kate was the one who'd called Abby out on her ungrateful behavior and told her—for lack of a better term—to pull her head in.

So as Abby sat at the table for the welcome party of Kate's mom, it was hard for her to watch someone be so rude to Kate.

To Abby, Kate was a saint. She was a sweet person—and Abby didn't like very many people. But she liked Kate. Helen...she did not.

"Are you close to Louise?" Helen asked her.

Abby nodded. "Yeah, I guess you could say that." Abby was uncomfortable, although she knew she had no right to feel that way. Being Louise's stepdaughter was always going to raise eyebrows. People could count, they could do the numbers. Them being mother and daughter did not add up. Even so, she hadn't expected to have it questioned so close to home.

"Do you have many things in common?" The woman fired questions non-stop.

"I guess...we work at the bookstore together, so we get to spend a lot of time with each other." Abby began working at Chapter Five almost a year ago now. She first started by going to the store after school and then built her hours up during the school breaks. She enjoyed the atmosphere at the store and liked being around books. To Abby, books were so much better than people. Her first after-school job was at the Dockside Café and it overwhelmed her. She didn't enjoy having to talk to so many people every single day. And it wasn't just that. It seemed to Abby that people were a lot calmer and nicer browsing for books than they were waiting for food.

"You work at a bookstore?" Helen asked.

Kate had once told Abby that the lifestyle in the Philippines and Carlton Bay were miles different. People who worked in customer service or retail were the ones who were unqualified—or, as one might put it, uneducated. Kate had loved the fact that in the United States, people could be whatever they wanted to be, pursue any career they wanted to, be it plumbing or dentistry, and you could still live a comfortable life. Abby was certain that Helen was looking down on her for working in a bookstore. She could feel it in the hairs that rose at the back of her neck. Abby wished the woman would stop talking to her. She stared at the bit of food stuck in between Helen's two front teeth, but said nothing about it. She wished Shelby was there. Shelby was much better with awkward conversations and small talk. "Mrs. Delaney owns a bookstore downtown," she said. "It's called Chapter Five."

"Mrs. Delaney?" Helen frowned. "So, you don't call her Mommy?"

"Huh?" Abby hated every minute of the conversation. Why is she talking to me? Please talk to someone else!

"Your stepmother," Helen said, "you don't call her your mother?"

Abby twisted her mouth and chewed on the inside of her cheek. Please stop talking to me, she thought. Abby glanced at Philip as if signaling him to help.

"Abby and Louise haven't been in each other's lives for very long," Philip offered. "They're still getting to know each other, but they do get along very well."

Thank God for Philip—literally. Thank you, Abby willed Philip to hear her thoughts.

"I always feel sorry for children who come from broken homes," Helen said. "You're lucky that your stepmother has taken you in," she told Abby. The woman had no filter. No filter at all.

Abby nodded. "I know." Is there no end to this woman's opinions? Helen was so different from Kate. It was difficult to think of them as mother and daughter. Kate was such a nice person; it was impossible not to like her. Over the last few years, Abby had looked to Kate as an older sister. "Kate helped me to see that," she added.

"Kate?" Helen seemed surprised and laughed a loud and hideous laugh that it actually hurt Abby's ears and chest. "Well, that's good to know. Kate is always so against everything I say, quite the disappointment to her father and I. Did you know that she came to the US against our wishes?"

Abby blinked. What did Helen want her to say? She couldn't think of anything to say, so she just shrugged.

"How old did you say you were?"

"Eighteen."

Helen nodded. "I can see why you get along with Kate. She was just like you at your age. Mind you, she still acts like she's eighteen," she shook her head with a tsk. "It's a shame. My friend's children had all gone on to be lawyers and doctors." Helen sighed, making no effort to mask her disapproval of Kate's lifestyle.

Abby said nothing and barely managed a smile.

Chapter 6

Sarah Gardner

Sarah followed Kate and Louise into the backyard. She could see that Helen was talking to Abby. *Poor girl*, she thought, knowing that Abby wasn't a big talker. Sarah set the cookies in the center of the table next to where Kate had put the cheesecake. "These lovely cookies were made by Abby," she said, casting a glance at the teenager. "And the cheesecake was made by Philip."

"Is all this for me?" Helen beamed. "How nice of you all to go out of your way for me."

Sarah was relieved by Helen's softened vibe. A bit of thanks and gratitude goes a long way. "Well," she began, "you are our best friend's mother, and we wanted you to know how happy we all are to have you with us."

"That's nice," Helen said, "but I've cut out sugar from my diet a long time ago. Sugar kills, you know." And just like that, the mood had shifted again.

"Surely a couple of small bites won't hurt," Sarah said with a smile. "Or maybe we can tempt you with just a cookie? Abby worked very hard on these for you."

"Oh, it's okay," Abby said. "I don't mind." Knowing Abby, she didn't care for the added attention.

"There—see?" Helen gestured at Abby. "She doesn't mind."

Kate tried to step in. "Ma, maybe you can have a small slice?"

"Oh—and I suppose you want me to die too?" Helen frowned. "Your father—bless his soul—he was the dessert man. Or did you forget that about him? If his heart hadn't killed him first, then the sugar would have gotten to him."

"Alright, that's enough bickering, ladies," Louise said. "No one needs to have dessert if they don't want to. Besides, you can't get a figure like Helen's from eating desserts, can you?"

"Finally," Helen sighed, "someone who understands."

Sarah watched how Louise laughed and joked along with Helen with such ease. She wished she could be like Louise and just carry on, but Helen was just so rude. Perhaps they were just two very different people.

"You should think about quitting sugar, you know," Helen turned her attention back to Kate. "It would certainly help you lose all that weight you've put on. And I guarantee you'll feel much better."

Sarah rolled her eyes. She did not like Helen, nor the way she was treating Kate. Sure, she was a hot woman—especially for a fifty-year-old. One could easily mistake Helen for someone Sarah's age. But her attitude was deplorable.

"Mommy, I want more." Noah held his empty plate up for everyone to see.

"I think you've had enough now, Noah," Sarah said. "That was quite a big slice you'd had."

"But I want more!" Noah demanded, his face smeared with cheesecake.

"I said, no more, Noah." Sarah glared at her middle child. Since Noah had started school, she's had trouble managing his behavior. He'd become demanding, selfish, and high-strung. The fact was, the school had called Sarah in to meet with his teacher too many times to count now. She really didn't want him to make a scene now. Not with Helen there. Not with her watching. Helen didn't know him well enough.

"More!" Noah shouted. "I want more!"

"Noah," Caleb tried, "your mom said you've had enough."

"But I want more!" Noah began to cry and then wail.

Sarah glanced at Helen, who she'd noticed was shaking her head. Was it disapproval? Her face annoyed Sarah. Who did this woman think she was? "Noah, that—is—enough," she said through gritted teeth.

"Noah can get a bit excitable at times," Louise turned to Helen.

"Mmm—yes, so I see," Helen said.

Helen's condescending tone grated Sarah. She got up and pushed her seat back. She made her way to where Noah sat, but before she could get to him, he jumped out of his seat and ran around the other side of the table. Sarah glanced at Caleb.

Caleb got up. "Noah—"

"But I want more," he whined. "I don't like you anymore," he yelled at Sarah and then ran next to Helen, climbing over her as he tried to reach for the cheesecake.

Kate tried pleading with him too. "Noah—please. Your mom said no and I think you—"

Without warning, Helen took Noah's wrist and spanked the top of his hand with a resounding smack. "No means no!"

Everyone around the table gasped.

Noah pulled his hand back in shock, and then big tears followed quickly.

Sarah stood frozen. Someone had just hit her child. Someone she barely knew. Someone she'd just met. They'd hit her child. Sarah took a deep breath and glared at Helen. She glanced at Kate.

All the color had drained from Kate's face. "Ma!"

"Someone had to stop him. Saying his name over and over will do nothing," Helen said. She motioned to Noah. "Look at him—he's stopped now, hasn't he?"

Sarah lost all cool. "I think you should leave," she said to Helen. "Kate,"—Sarah looked at her—"I'm sorry."

Kate nodded. "Of course—no, I'm, I'm sorry," Kate stammered before she got up from her seat. "Ma, let's go."

"What?" The confusion on Helen's face irritated Sarah.

She couldn't believe the woman had the gall to feign confusion, as if she hadn't done anything wrong. "Louise?" Sarah didn't know why she'd turned to Louise. Was it to ask for help? To ask if what she'd done was wrong? A million thoughts raced through her mind.

"I'll take the kids inside," Caleb said, making the first move.

"Right—let's all just relax. I think we all need to take a step back. Everyone's tired and it's been a long day." Louise—she could fix it. Louise could fix anything.

Sarah clenched her jaw; her breathing, heavy. She could feel the sting of tears in her eyes. That was the first time she had felt anger in a long while. Her hands shook as she cleared the table. "The party's over," she muttered.

Philip placed a hand over Sarah's. "Let me take care of this," he said calmly. "You go on inside and—"

Sarah didn't let him finish. She nodded, grateful for his control and composure. She watched as Kate, Adam, and Helen disappeared through the kitchen door. It had all happened without warning. What was she supposed to do? Was it okay that some stranger had hit her child? What did it mean for her friendship with Kate? What a disaster. She wished she'd never offered to host a welcome party in the first place.

Chapter 7

Louise Delaney

After Kate and her mom left, Louise put the kettle on and prepared two cups of tea—one for Sarah and the other for herself. Caleb, Philip, and Abby had taken the children to the park to blow some energy off. She felt for Sarah, but she also felt for Kate. No one could have predicted what had happened that afternoon.

Louise knew how much Kate had looked forward to seeing her mother. She'd spoken fondly of her recounting memories from long ago. It seemed to Louise that some, if not most, of those memories might have been romanticized. Helen was fun to be with—but you had to be on the same wavelength to appreciate her company.

Louise thought about when her own daughter was a toddler. She had never—not once—raised her hand to Madison. Neither had Warren. It just wasn't their way. It didn't mean that she didn't get frustrated or angry. What parent didn't? She'd lost her patience with Madison many times, but striking had never been a method of punishment in their home. She and Warren took things away and implemented time-outs. It was funny...despite the absence of spanking, Louise was estranged from her daughter. She sniffed at the irony.

"How are you feeling?" she asked Sarah as she set the tray down on the table. Louise looked up at the sky. The night was still early. Louise knew that Sarah had a tendency to overthink things, dwelling on matters that one might advise letting go of. She knew Sarah would be harboring some emotions inside of her, and it was best to encourage her to just let it all out.

Sarah shook her head. She sat back, leaning on the garden chair, a hand to her mouth, her lips curled in. "I don't know." Sarah turned to face her. "Do you think I overreacted?" Her face was distraught.

Louise sighed, careful to choose the right words. "It was unexpected. I can tell you that much."

"I mean—who does that?" She furiously wiped at her tears. Sarah was always the first one to tears. Some people were just quick to tears and Sarah was one of them. "I'm just so angry! What a presumptuous woman!"

"I can understand why you're angry." Louise poured the tea out for both of them. "In fact, I was thinking back to when Madison was a child. Hitting just wasn't something we did."

"I have never,"—Sarah choked back on her tears—"hit any of my children! Never!"

"Honey," Louise soothed, "I know you're upset—"

"I'm more than upset, Louise! How could she do that? I wanted to lunge at her!" Sarah growled.

Louise had never seen Sarah so angry before. Frustrated, maybe. Upset, definitely. But never angry to the point of violence. Fair enough. She was a mother. And mothers were fierce when it came to protecting their children, hence the phrase Mama Bear.

"What am I gonna do?" Sarah sighed, a worried frown on her face.

Louise thought of what she would have done had it been her child. "Why don't you sleep on it first? Clear your head and things will come to you in the morning."

"What about Kate?"

"What about her?" Louise took a sip of her tea.

"Do you think she's upset with me? I mean...I asked her mom to leave my house." Sarah was torn.

"Well, her mom hit your kid, darling. I think Kate understands. She's a smart cookie—and a mother herself."

They sat in silence for a few moments, when Sarah looked up from her cup. "Do you think there's something wrong with Noah?" she asked softly.

There it was. The question that many have secretly wanted to raise, but were cautious not to—herself included. Louise listened.

Sarah sniffed and used the back of her hand to wipe her nose. "They've called me to meet with the school teacher so many times. I mean—I just don't know what to do." Sarah shook her head. "It wasn't like this with Liam. There was never anything of this sort. You remember, don't you?" Sarah looked to Louise expectantly. "With Liam, it's always meetings about how talented he is,"—Sarah shook her head—"or how kind and giving he is. With Noah, it always seems to be bad news."

Louise knew about the teacher meetings. At first, they thought it was just Noah trying to adjust to his new environment. Going to big school, after all, is a big change for children and everyone copes in their own way. But when things didn't improve over time, Sarah had begun to worry. "All children are unique, Sarah. You can't compare Liam's experience to Noah's."

Sarah bit her bottom lip and stared into the distance. "I know that...I do. But why is he so—I can't even describe it. He's just so full of energy. All the time. It's boundless! He refuses to share, and he doesn't know how to play with the other kids. He always ends up in a fight with someone. Surely that's not normal?"

"What is normal anyway?" Louise could see where Sarah's fears were coming from and she wished she could give her more advice, but she had nothing.

"Do you think it's me? Have I failed him as a mother? Is there something I'm not doing right? What if it's hereditary? I mean...I suffered from depression. That's a mental illness, right? And what about Zoe?" Questions spewed out of her.

"I think—" Louise paused for a thought. How could she put it? "Every parent blames themselves for whatever their kids go through. That's always the first response." Louise knew all about carrying blame. And she knew about guilt. She'd carried both for many years as her relationship with her own daughter had deteriorated down to a permanent estrangement, with Madison on the opposite side of the world in New Zealand with the granddaughter she will never get to know. "I know that I have blamed myself for my relationship with Madison—or the absence of one."

Sarah shifted in her seat. "Do you ever think of her?"

Louise smiled weakly. "All the time."

"Why have you never reached out to her?" Sarah asked. "If I'm—I mean, you don't have to tell me if you don't want to. I'm sorry," Sarah shook her head.

Louise sighed. Why hasn't she reached out to Madison? She could ask the same of her daughter—why hasn't Madison made any attempt to reach out to her? She'd tried. In fact, she'd tried many times in the past. "I guess, there comes a time when you realize that it's just the way things are." Louise shook her head. Did she really mean that? No. Not a day went by that she didn't think of Madison. It was impossible not to. It's true what they say, it doesn't matter how old your children get; they'll always be your babies.

Chapter 8

Kate Morgan

Kate sat on the edge of Helen's bed and watched as her mother unpacked her bags. She was afraid to speak; to question her and challenge her behavior. "I can't believe you did that," she said after a long time stewing over it. Her voice, soft and timid.

Helen looked up from the opened suitcase sprawled over the bed. "Did what?"

Kate took a deep breath in. "That you smacked Noah."

Helen shook her head. "I didn't smack him. I merely gave him a tap on his hand. He needed to know that what he was doing wasn't okay."

"That was a smack. We all saw and heard it." Kate's heart was racing. The last thing she wanted was a confrontation. She hated confrontation of any sort.

"It was not a smack," Helen maintained. "People are just so sensitive these days. They get offended too easily. The boy was misbehaving. No one else was doing anything, and he needed to be disciplined."

"Not by you!" Kate argued. "He's my best friend's son—I mean...why would you do something like that?" Kate was beside

60

herself. She didn't know how she could face Sarah after what her mother had done. "I don't even know how I'm going to look Sarah in the face. What am I going to say to her? I'm sorry my mom hit your son?"

"Why do you have to say anything at all?"

Kate snorted. "You're joking, right?" Shock couldn't even begin to describe what Kate was feeling. She couldn't believe that her own mother could be so callous.

"No—does it look like I'm joking? That woman—"

"Sarah."

"Whatever," Helen said dismissively. "Sarah should learn how to control her own children. That's how children grow up to be selfish little brats without a conscience."

"He's six," Kate argued.

"And I'm fifty—so what?"

"Exactly! You're fifty. Why would you even stoop to the level of a six-year-old? What were you thinking?"

"That's not the point I'm making, Katherine."

"Then please—by all means—enlighten me, because I'm dying to know."

Helen stood upright. "Katherine Ann Valdez—"

"It's Morgan." Kate knew she was in for it. She'd never once won an argument against her mother. No one ever does. It was one of the many things Kate did not inherit from her. Helen was a vocal woman. She said whatever was on her mind and she did not hold back. Kate once watched her tear a server to shreds for an unsatisfactory meal at a fast-food restaurant—not even a fine-dining restaurant. The manager came out to intercede and Kate watched in awe Helen managed to get the whole bill crossed off, rendering their meal free. It wasn't until Kate was much older that she realized that what she'd witnessed wasn't something to be proud of. Many more realizations followed. Unfortunately for Kate, vowing never to be so petty and unscrupulous had meant becoming somewhat of a doormat. Kate was nothing like her mother.

"Is it? Because one moment you're telling me you've divorced your husband and even have the audacity to pick me up at the airport with your lover, and now you're telling me it's Morgan. What is it?" she spat. "And as for Sarah—your best friend—perhaps if she focused more on her children than her boyfriend, then other people wouldn't have to do it for her."

"Ma! What—" Kate's hands trembled in anger.

"Well, isn't it true? Didn't her husband just die? And she has another man between the sheets already? Has she no shame?" Righteousness echoed in Helen's words. A devout Catholic, she went to mass every day at 6:00am; converting Kate's father to the same practice. Kate had heard the story of how she was conceived in prayer and service to the Lord. Kate's father had wanted a child. It was only when he'd agreed to attend daily mass that Helen had agreed.

"That's not fair," Kate said. "You know nothing about her." She struggled to find the words to defend her friend. They escaped her just as they did every time Kate found herself in any dispute. Helen, on the other hand, was quick with words—some might even call her witty. She was good at crosswords, no one had ever beaten her at Scrabble; she devoured books and was a champion debater in high school.

"I've seen enough to know that she was one of those who convinced you that getting a divorce was the thing to do. Am I right? That just goes to show what values they have."

"He hit me!" Kate cried. She could no longer hold it in. "Evan hit me! He abused me! Why aren't you on my side?"

Helen glared at her. "All marriages have problems, Kate. Don't go making yourself out to be a martyr."

"A martyr?" Kate was disgusted in her mother. "What would you have me do? You'd rather that I stayed with an abusive alcoholic?"

"He's off the alcohol now, isn't he?" Helen pointed out. "For better or worse. Those were your vows. It was your responsibility to help him get through it. There were times when I wanted to give up on your father too, you know. It happens in all marriages."

Kate sensed there was no reasoning with her mother. Nothing she could say would make her mother see things from her perspective. She felt betrayed by her mother's lack of empathy for what she had gone through. "But, I'm your daughter—"

"And I expected more from you. You should go back to him and lay in the bed you've made."

Kate looked into her mother's enlarged eyes. Saliva gathered at the sides of Helen's mouth. That wasn't her mother. No. That was someone else. Who was she? Kate held her tears back. She refused to let her mother get to her.

"Well?"

"Never mind," Kate said, her heart crushed. "Forget it."

"No!" Helen shouted. "I will not forget it! Is this what America has done to you? You've forgotten all your values? You betrayed the sacred vows of marriage—vows you made before God. And you dare to speak to your mother like this." Helen placed her hands on her hips. "Who are you? What's happened to you?"

Kate felt her sense of self dwindling by the second. "I should ask the same of you," she mumbled.

"You will not speak to me like that!" Helen's voice was hair-raising. "Do you hear me? Your father would be so disappointed in you if he were here right now."

"I am a disappointment anyway, aren't I?" Kate shouted. "That's what I am, right?"

Helen pursed her lips. "This is your fault," she hissed. "If you hadn't left to follow some stupid fantasy, then your father wouldn't have died of a broken heart and he would still be with us. He would still be with me!"

Kate clenched her jaw. "Are you—" Kate couldn't believe it. She closed her eyes and exhaled out of her nose. "Are you actually blaming me for Daddy's death?"

"He missed you, Kate! You were his little princess, and what did you do? You deserted him." Helen spat the words out, cutting Kate like a hot knife to butter—smooth, clean, and intentional.

Kate was trembling. This couldn't be happening. Tears stung her eyes. Stand up for yourself, Kate. Tell her this isn't okay! Kate balled her hands into fists.

"What?" Helen went right up to Kate's face. "You want to hit me? Go on!" she challenged. "Go ahead—hit me!" Helen's left nostril quivered. It was a sign of anger. Kate had seen it many times before.

"Stop it!" Kate couldn't take it anymore. She wanted to hit her mother. Kate had never had such violent thoughts, but she wanted so much to shut her mother up.

"You left your father...for what, Kate? For love,"—Helen raised an eyebrow—"isn't that what you said? Well, why don't you show me the love?" Helen looked around the room with an exaggeration that fueled Kate's anger. "Why don't you show me the love that you have left your father for, because I sure don't see it!"

Kate glared at her mother.

"What?" her mother glared back at her. "What?" she screamed. "You want to send me away? You wouldn't dare. This is your fault. You've made a mistake, Kate. Look around you...you're nothing but a slave to these white people!"

Kate turned on heels and slammed the door behind her. Tears streamed down her face as her hands shook with anger.

She went to check on Adam in his bedroom. He was fast asleep in his crib. She wiped the tears off her face and reached in to touch him—her baby, her angel.

Kate leaned against the crib and slid to the floor. She strained to breathe, each wave getting caught in her chest. A low moan escaped from her throat. Kate opened her mouth, careful not to let the sound of her cries out. Why was this happening? Seven years.

Chapter 9

Sarah Gardner

"Are you okay?" Caleb asked Sarah after everyone had gone. He put his hands on her shoulders, giving her a gentle massage.

Sarah put a hand on his. "I just can't believe she did that, you know?" Misery loves company. Everyone knows that. Sarah wondered if she was blowing things out of proportion. As it was, she was known for her tendency to do just that.

Caleb pulled a chair out and sat next to her at the dining table. He rubbed at the stubble on his chin. "Yeah—that was pretty surreal. It shocked me when it happened, but I wasn't sure what to do. I should have done something, but it was Kate's mom, you know? I wasn't going to jump on tiny a fifty-year-old woman."

Over the last year or so, Caleb had become a real part of their family. He was a very important male figure in the lives of the children—and Sarah's. "I'm sorry I didn't get to announce our good news." They were supposed to tell everyone that Caleb was finally moving in with the family as Sarah's partner, instead of the male nanny that he was when they'd first met. They'd come a long way, and he'd put up with a lot of Sarah's crazies the way she knew no one else would.

"There'll be another time," he said. "Don't worry about it." Caleb was an easy-going guy. Sarah admired the way he never let things get the better of him. "If it won't matter in a year's time, then don't waste your heart on it," he always said.

Sarah sighed. "Caleb,"—she hesitated—"you and I...we both agree that there's no hitting in this family, right?"

Caleb frowned thoughtfully. "Do you think I would ever hit the kids? Or you?"

Sarah felt bad that she was even raising the topic. But having Helen hit Noah made her realize that they hadn't actually talked about how they wanted to raise the kids. The children were hers—and Adam's. She needed to know that she and Caleb were on the same page. Hitting was not something she approved of. "It's just—"

"No, I get it," he said.

Sarah nodded. "I don't think Kate ever thought that Evan could become violent."

"I can understand that," he said. Caleb leaned forward. He clasped his hands together and sighed. "Sarah—I love you," he said. "And I love the kids. There are no two ways about it. I don't believe in hitting children. In fact, I don't condone any kind of violence. I will never raise a hand to the kids—do you hear me?"

"I'm sorry." Sarah looked into his eyes. Caleb was the kindest, most gentle man she's known. Even with a tattoo along his arm, Caleb did not look the least bit antagonizing. "I know you would never hurt the kids."

"They're your children and you just want to make sure they're in safe hands. I will never ever do anything to hurt them...or you."

Sarah rubbed her face. Fatigue overcame her.

"Come here," Caleb said as he pulled her into an embrace. "I love you. And I love the kids."

"I love you too." Sarah melted into his arms and closed her eyes.

"Are we expecting anyone?" Caleb asked at the sound of a knock on the front door.

Sarah shook her head. She looked up at the clock on the kitchen wall. It was almost 8:00pm.

"You stay here; I'll get it."

When Caleb returned, Kate was with him.

"Hi Sarah." Kate smiled.

"Kate..." A small curve formed at the corner of Sarah's mouth.

"I hope I haven't come at a bad time," Kate said.

"Do you want a cup of tea?" Sarah offered and glanced at Caleb, who'd already started filling the kettle.

"I'd love one," Kate said.

"I'll take care of it, honey," Sarah told Caleb.

"I'll check on the kids then," Caleb said as he gave Sarah a peck on the check. He placed a hand on Kate's shoulder and gave it a squeeze. "I'll see you tomorrow, I'm sure."

"About what happened...how are you feeling?" Kate asked.

Sarah shrugged. "I was a bit shocked. Is she really like that? I'm sorry I asked her to leave."

Kate nodded. "It took me by surprise too," she said. Kate reached for Sarah's hand. "I am so, so sorry, Sarah," she said.

As much as Sarah wanted to wave everything off, she couldn't. She pulled her hand away slowly. "It wasn't your fault."

"But she's my mom and I brought her—"

"You weren't to know."

Kate shook her head and leaned back in her chair. "She never hit me as a child, so what she did to Noah was a surprise to me. I remember, there was one time—when I was about eight or nine—I broke a bottle of maple syrup that my mom's sister had sent from California. It was an unopened bottle. She got so mad. She made me kneel on the kitchen counter with my arms stretched out to the sides."

Sarah listened. Orphaned at a young age, Sarah had spent many years in the system, experiencing all manners of discipline. She shook her head as a wave of memories came to her. She'd been at the Johnson's home for just over a week. Sarah was thirteen, and she'd just started her periods. No one had ever told her about it; in fact, she thought she was sick or even dying. She'd put on two pairs of underwear, but the blood seeped through on to the Johnson's brand-new sofa, anyway.

Sarah recalled Mr. Johnson's face when he saw the fresh stain, as she got up to get him a bottle of beer from the fridge. He made her pull her pants down. "Take your panties off too," he yelled. Sarah pleaded with him, apologizing. She felt sick, humiliated. She looked to Mrs. Johnson for help, but she turned the other way. Before she knew it, Sarah could feel the sting of the thick leather belt against her flesh. One. Two. Three. Four. Five.

She stayed with them for eight months; never given a choice.

The next family she moved in with were different, but Sarah kept her guard up. She still remembered the day when her foster parents asked her if she wanted to join their family. "Do you mean forever?" she'd asked. It was the day of her fifteenth birthday, not long to go before she aged out. Sarah was one of the lucky ones.

Kate continued. "I don't know how long I had to kneel on the counter for, but I remember was how upset I was. When I broke the bottle, I ran up to tell my mom what I'd done. Honesty's the best policy, right?" Kate looked up at Sarah. "I didn't expect to be punished like that. But Sarah..."

"Kate...it's okay," Sarah said. She didn't like the memories that the conversation was dredging. "Really."

Kate's shoulders slumped forward. "I just don't want it to get awkward between us...you know?"

"I know," Sarah smiled. "It won't. I promise."

Chapter 10

Louise Delaney

Back at home, Louise and Abby went into the kitchen for a nightcap—a cup of green tea for Louise and a hot chocolate for Abby.

Abby told Louise about what had happened when they'd left her to go into the kitchen and how Helen had thrown dozens of questions that had made her feel uncomfortable. "What did you think about what happened today at Sarah's?"

Louise took a sip of her tea. "To be honest, I was quite surprised when Helen struck Noah."

"I know, right? I was so mad at her," Abby said. "I mean, even if I didn't have the best mother—at least she never hit me. I've been babysitting those kids for ages and I'd never ever do such a thing."

"Mmm..." Louise said thoughtfully. There were other things on her mind, but she understood why everyone was so upset by what had happened.

"Do you like her? That Helen lady?"

"She's alright," Louise said. "I'm sure she's a nice person. She's probably as surprised as we were that she did what she did. I think we just need to give her a chance. She'd been bombarded with people and rowdy kids after a long flight. And to be honest, not everyone likes kids."

"That's true. But still, there's something about her that I don't like, especially how she talks to Kate. She was real rude! Like, super rude."

"Kate is the one I'm most worried about. It was supposed to be a welcome party, and she was so excited for her mother to arrive. She must be quite upset right now."

"Well, I don't see what she was excited about. It was like...I don't know. Like, her mom kept telling her off. I actually felt a bit embarrassed for Kate."

"Yes, I did notice that."

"I think everyone did," Abby sniffed. "My allergies are going crazy. I must have sneezed, like, fifty times today."

"Let's see how the next few days go. Give the woman a chance to rest and recover," Louise said. "Have you taken anything for your allergies?"

"Yup!" Abby nodded. "Did Philip say anything about it?" she asked. Over the last year, Abby had grown closer to Philip. Abby had even joked about calling him dad. The three of them had become a little family—make it four, counting Abby's friend, Shelby, who was at the house almost as often as Philip, if not more.

"Oh, you know Philip," Louise said. "He likes to see the good in everyone. He thinks that maybe there's a cultural gap of sorts there. Perhaps that's how they discipline children in the Philippines."

"Didn't he spend time in the Philippines? He should know what it's like then." Abby thought for a moment. "Do you think

Kate would be the same with Adam? Like, would she hit him or something?"

"Goodness, no," Louise said. She knew Kate very well. "I don't think Kate has a mean bone in her body. She looked about as surprised as we all were."

Abby sipped on her hot chocolate. "Do you know why Sarah cries so much? Like, she does it all the time—you know, like, if things don't go her way or something; or, like, if she's sad, she cries."

"Sarah is...." Louise hesitated. She was glad that she and Abby were able to talk to each other; unlike the early days when Abby had first moved in. Back then, Louise only ever seemed to say the wrong thing. About Sarah—Abby wasn't wrong; but she wondered about how she could she explain it to her. "Sarah's been through a lot. I think you know that. But sometimes—well, actually, often—people are the way they are because of what's happened to them in the past." Louise took a sip of her tea. "Have you ever heard the saying—the best predictor of future behavior is past behavior?"

Abby shook her head.

"Our experiences shape who we are. Some wounds take longer to heal than others. It's just one of the many imperfections of humanity."

"So something happened to her in the past, so now she cries a lot?"

"It's not that simple, but in essence, yes."

"I guess...but I mean, I've had things happen to me in the past and I hate crying. Like, get over yourself, and just move on." Abby finished the rest of hot chocolate. "But don't tell Sarah I said that, okay?" Abby made a face and grinned. "I'm going to go to bed now," Abby said as she got up and pushed her chair in. "Can I help you with anything before I go?"

Louise wanted to point out that Abby herself was a fighter because she'd had to learn how to do so from a very young age. But she didn't—it wasn't the time for it. "No thanks," she said. "You go on and I'll tidy up down here. Leave your cup in the sink."

"You sure?"

It was nice to see how much Abby had changed. When Louise first met her, the girl had a lot of anger and couldn't properly express herself. But in the last few years, they'd been able to work through things together. Abby had been a blessing in Louise's life—believe it or not. She was very fond of the girl and was proud to be her stepmom. Her presence had made life a little more fun, a little more interesting. Parenting at sixty-one differed greatly from parenting at twenty. Louise had more sense as an adult...or so she felt. There were so many things she wanted to teach Abby. To prepare her for real life, to impart her knowledge and whatever wisdom she'd gained in the last six decades. "I am—go on," she said. "Have fun/. Do whatever you teenagers do at this time of the night."

"Eew," Abby wrinkled her nose. "What does that mean?"

"Nothing," Louise laughed. "I'll be heading up shortly myself."

"I'm gonna give Shelby a call and see what she's up to."

"Where is she staying tonight?" Louise asked. Shelby didn't have an easy life at home. Her parents did not approve of her lifestyle, seeing as Shelby's real name was Toby—more specifically, Tobias.

"I don't know. Should I ask her?"

Louise nodded. "Tell her I'd rather she stays here than out on the streets again." Shelby was Abby's best friend. Though Louise found their friendship a bit strange, she was happy that Abby was happy. Louise liked how they were able to lean on each other, much like she did with Kate and Sarah.

"I will," Abby said as she disappeared through the living room.

Louise stared at her cup. She hadn't been feeling well and had been to a few doctors already—second, third, and even fourth opinions. Something wasn't right; she could feel it, but she hadn't told anyone about it just yet. Why worry them? She felt a bit...hazy.

Her thoughts moved to Helen—an unexpected firecracker. But just the same, she hoped that they could all be friends. She wanted, more than anything, for Kate to be happy.

Louise heard a sound go off. A melody—what was it? She looked around, hoping to find its source. And then...it stopped.

That's odd, Louise thought and frowned.

But then it went off again.

The sound was coming from her purse; she was sure of it. Louise looked inside. "The phone!" She laughed and shook her head as she pulled out her mobile phone. The screen showed Kate was calling. "Hi," she said when she picked up.

"Are you home?" Kate asked.

"Yes—"

"Can I come over?"

For a moment, Louise was flustered. She must have changed the ring tone at some point because she didn't recognize the sound. Never mind. "Sure, I'll open the door for you. See you in a minute." Louise made her way to the front door. Living across from each other was handy, and she enjoyed how they could all just pop into each other's houses. Louise had done so herself, many times. She opened the door to Kate walking up the driveway. "Hi!" she said again.

JUST AS LOUISE HAD thought, Kate was upset. She'd wanted to talk about what happened at the party. "Don't worry about it," she told Kate. "It will pass." The truth was, Louise didn't want to talk. She didn't want to discuss anyone's hurt feelings, or share any words of comfort. Was that selfish of her? No. She had other stuff going on, and Louise was mentally exhausted. Literally. She'd had enough of thinking, of processing. All she wanted was to get into a nice warm bath and soak the day away. She could already smell the vanilla and rose bath salts she'd recently bought from the Dockside market. Louis Armstrong serenading her in the background sounded just like what the doctor ordered.

"She's different," Kate said.

Louise didn't want to ask who was different, but she did. "Who's different?"

"My mom. We had an argument tonight, so I left."

Her mom—Heather. No, Helen. Louise could feel sleep coming on and she was getting slightly irritated. "What about Adam?" Louise asked.

"He's asleep." Kate told Louise about what had transpired between Helen and herself. "I don't understand why she's so antagonizing. It's just not like her."

"Has she not always been like this? It's not a personality thing?" People didn't just up and change their ways. That's not how things worked. It was not how people worked, anyway. The best predictor of future behavior is past behavior, she thought for the second time that night.

"No...I mean, sure, we've had arguments in the past. But that's all normal mother and daughter stuff. There's just something off about her."

"Give her some time." That's all she could say. Everyone else had time. Everyone except her. Louise didn't have the time or patience to spare. She wanted to give into herself. For once, she wanted the night to be about her. She's always been the kind and caring one. Not now. No. Louise wanted to be selfish—to think of herself only. There was a name for it. She just couldn't remember what it was.

"I don't know," Kate faltered.

Louise wanted to comfort her, but she knew that there were times—often—when people romanticized the past. As far as she was concerned, she'd done the same with Warren. There was a time after Warren had died when, in her eyes, they'd had a beautiful relationship. When the cloud of grief lifted, she began to see things with more clarity. It wasn't all Warren's fault, mind you—may his soul rest in peace. She had a lot to do with him straying. She'd pushed him away and straight into the arms of a floozy in Portland. No, Louise shook her head. There was even a time when, dared she say it, that she was glad to be on her own, living her life. "Relationships are complicated," she said. "People change. We may not always know the reason behind the change, but it happens."

"I really hope this doesn't affect my relationship with Sarah."

"With Sarah?"

"Yes, I went to see her—to apologize for my mom's behavior—"

"I'll stop you right there, if I may," Louise interjected. "It was your mom's behavior—not yours. I doubt Sarah will blame you for something your mother has done. You'll see, it'll all blow over in a few days. Don't get yourself worked up over nothing. Sarah knows better than to put this on you."

"I hope so." Kate bit her bottom lip.

"I know so." Louise could understand where Kate's fears were coming from. Before they'd all become friends, Kate was alone most of the time. She'd spent days and nights at home just waiting for her husband to get back from work. And when he did, she'd spent it catering to his every little need. Not that she was to blame for how Evan had treated her—no, of course not. That was the mistake that so many people make; to blame the victim for the behaviors of the abuser. As it turned out, Evan was an alcoholic. Going to AA and keeping himself steady on the wagon was a good thing—for everyone; for Kate, Adam, and himself.

"Where's Abby?" Kate asked.

"In her bedroom. She's just gone up for the night. Probably on the phone with Shelby."

"Is she working tomorrow?"

Abby had begun doing part-time work at the bookstore when she was in high school. It gave her a sense of routine. Home, school, and work. Sometimes, when the store was busy, Shelby came in to help too. Louise was glad to be able to offer Shelby a safe place—or at least a place where she could feel safe. After she graduated from high school, she spent more hours at the store. "Yes, she's working full time until end of the summer break, before heading back to college."

"I've been thinking about coming back to work," Kate said. Before she'd given birth to Adam, Kate had worked part time at the bookstore. It was after she'd left Evan. "Now that my mom is here, I can probably leave Adam with her and focus more on work."

"Do you think you're ready to do that?"

"Well, when Abby goes back to college, after the summer break, you'll be on your own."

"I don't mind—I can keep it going until you're back and ready. Shelby's not going to college, so I'm happy for her to continue helping out. Maybe spend some time with your mom first and see how things work out."

"I suppose you're right."

If she didn't know any better, Louise would say that Kate was looking to go back to work to avoid her mother. But it's only been a day. "Do you think she'll like it here?" Louise asked.

"Maybe—I don't see why not. I mean, there's nothing left for her in the Philippines. So really, there was no reason for her to remain there. Coming here was the best thing for her to do."

"Well, see how things go with her and then you can decide." Louise hoped, for Kate's sake, that things would work out with her mother.

"Thanks, Louise. You always know what to do."

Louise laughed. "Trust me, darling—I don't." Thoughts raced through her mind. She felt a tingling pain in her knee from when she'd fallen earlier that night. She hadn't told anyone about it the pain though. They'd only make a fuss, and she really didn't feel like having anyone fuss over her. Old age was catching up on her and she could feel it. Darned thing, it was. The wrinkles around her eyes—the ones that everyone so politely referred to as laugh lines—gave it away. Even her hands betrayed her, with their wrinkled lines staring right back up at her. No amount of cream rubbed them off. Old age...where was that fountain of youth that everyone talked about? Now that life is finally going well for her, old age sneaks up fast. It's true what they say, youth is wasted on the young. Bugger.

Self-care! That was the word she was looking for. It wasn't about being selfish. Louise was anything but selfish. "Now go on and get your butt back home," Louise said, leading Kate by the shoulders. She wanted to put in some time for self-care, and she was determined not to let anything keep her from it.

Fall

The purpose of life is to live it, to taste experience to the utmost, to reach out eagerly and without fear for newer and richer experience.

~Eleanor Roosevelt

Chapter 11

Kate Morgan

The rest of summer had gone by with Kate pretending everything was well. Between the two of them, Kate and Helen had shared some light moments of laughter and reminiscing about the past. But the moments were sparse; some short-lived. Kate never seemed to know what triggered her mother's moods just as that one weekend, when Kate sat on the sofa clipping Adam's fingernails. "You're such a good boy, Adam," Kate cooed.

"I'm so in awe of you, Kate," Helen had said.

"Hmm?" Kate didn't look up, taking much care as she snipped Adam's tiny nails. "What do you mean?"

"When you were a baby, I was so afraid of cutting your nails. There was even one time I'd accidently cut you by the skin." Helen groaned at the memory. "My goodness, how you cried! I felt so bad that I'd hurt you."

Kate laughed. "Well, he's a good boy." She looked up at her mother. "Just look at him." Kate held up his teeny hand in hers. "Besides, didn't I have a nanny to do that? I remember you telling me that my nanny was a nurse."

"Yes, and she was a good nurse too. Very experienced."

"You didn't really have to do it on your own then. You had great help around you." She should have anticipated what was coming. She should have known.

Helen sat upright. "I won't apologize for having the money to hire a nurse to look after you, Kate. In fact, you should consider yourself privileged to have been raised by a qualified nurse."

Kate stopped clipping Adam's nails and looked up at Helen. "Did I say something wrong?"

"Just because you're in America now, you think you're so high and mighty," Helen hissed. "You're so arrogant! What happened to you? Your head is so big, I'm surprised you can walk through the doors in this house."

For the life of her, Kate couldn't figure out what had triggered Helen's mood. And that's the way it had been throughout summer. Kate would say something—goodness knows what it might have been—and Helen would latch on to it for dear life. As for Kate, she'd defaulted to withdrawing to her room, as if it wasn't her house or that she wasn't a grown woman. It had gotten so bad one day that Kate hid in the closet and wept...like she did when she was just a teen.

Helen had a way with people. She knew what to say—when to say it and how to say it—to get exactly what she wanted. It was a skill that she put to use at her pleasure. In fact, Helen had even made up with Sarah for what had happened on the night of her welcome dinner, saying that she was tired from the long flight and was upset to learn that Kate had gone ahead with the divorce and was now seeing Mark. Unsurprisingly, Sarah had given the all clear, saying all was forgiven and forgotten.

What was surprising, though, was that Helen had also started talking to Mark; albeit they were a long way from being good friends.

For the most part, Helen had taken to staying home. The drama and theatrics, no longer obvious to others, were reserved for Kate, who truly felt the brunt of Helen's presence.

"Who's my handsome *apo*? Who's my handsome grandson?" Helen cooed, stroking Adam's wispy hair. On a more positive note, Helen's relationship with Adam had blossomed. Kate enjoyed seeing her mother and son become close. Wherever Helen went, Adam followed like a shadow. "When are you going to shave his hair, Kate?"

Kate shrugged. After the shock phone call she'd received on Adam's birthday, shaving his hair lost its ranking on her list of priorities. "I guess I won't anymore. We'd missed his one-year shave *and* the second year—do we still need to?" The truth was, it had slipped her mind.

"That goes without saying. You have to if you want his hair to grow thick and beautiful. Look at your hair, it's so nice. I don't even know why you always tie it up in the messy bun. It just makes you look dirty, and it doesn't do you any favors. You have a round face, remember? You got that from your father's side of the family, I'm afraid."

Self-conscious, Kate pulled her ponytail off. She loved her hair, and once upon a time, she saw it as her crowning glory. But since she'd had Adam, it was just more practical to tie it, keeping it away from her face.

"Besides, there's nothing worse than a man with thinning hair," Helen said with a laugh. "We don't want to lose our hair while we're young, do we?" she asked, speaking to Adam who looked back at her with such love. "He's going to thank you for it when he gets older."

"I'll have a think about it," Kate said as she joined them at the table for breakfast. Kate reached for a slice of toast and spread a healthy layer of butter over it. There was nothing quite like bread straight from the toaster, slathered in butter, almond butter—which Kate had just recently discovered—and honey.

"My goodness, Kate!" Helen's face contorted with disgust. "That's a heart attack on a plate, if I've ever seen one."

Kate rolled her eyes. She'd grown used to her mother's quips, but it didn't make them easier to swallow. "It's not like I have it every day."

"Still, you need to pay attention to what you put in your body," Helen said. "I was a fitness instructor, remember? I know what I'm talking about."

"Yes, yes, yes...everyone knows you were a fitness instructor. Now, can I please enjoy my breakfast?"

"It's your body," Helen said disapprovingly, just as Kate was going to take a bite. "Speaking of which—have you thought about what you're going to do about the weight you've put on? I think it's time for you to consider exercising now. It will be harder for you to lose all that weight as time goes on."

"Ma! Please!" Kate sighed and rolled her eyes. Her mother had always had a nice body. Helen was one of those people who could eat anything and not put a single pound on. Kate, on the other hand, always had to pay close attention to what she put in her mouth—or rather, her belly and hips. Growing up, Helen had made sure that Kate knew she had an apple-shaped body.

"You may have nice legs," she'd said, "but you're prone to gaining weight around the stomach. And don't forget about your arms."

"Okay, *bahala ka*! It's up to you." Helen pouted and turned her attention back to Adam.

"You're right. It is up to me," Kate said, finally taking a bite of her buttered toast. "And it's not like I haven't been trying to lose the baby weight. Everyone says it will take time."

"Time that won't be helped by shoving lard in your body." Helen laughed maniacally at her own joke. "Did you wear jeans after you gave birth? I told you to wear jeans, remember? It would have been like an instant girdle."

Kate sighed and dropped the toast on her plate. She'd lost her appetite. "You know, I was thinking that it might be time for me to go back to work."

"Oh?"

"Yes," Kate said. "I don't have a lot of money saved up and now that there are two of us here, that means double the groceries, electricity. You know...double of everything."

Helen's mouth turned into a frown.

"I don't mean anything bad by it, Ma," Kate added quickly upon noticing her mother's face. "It's just the reality of things."

"I wouldn't be here if your father were still alive, you know? Is that reality enough for you?"

Kate's shoulders slumped. "I know—that's not what I meant. Really, I was just—" Kate shook her head. "You know what? Never mind. Forget I said anything."

"Are you saying it's too complicated for me to understand? Because I've been a housewife and that I simply couldn't understand what you mean?"

"Oh my gosh!" Kate's palms stung when she slammed the table with both hands. "Can we please just have a conversation without arguing? I mean, seriously! Not everything is about you!" Her heart banged against her chest. "I'm going to look for full-time work so that I can support this household. That's all I'm saying."

"Fine. You're the boss."

Kate clicked her tongue. If there was anything she'd learned over the summer, it was that Helen preferred to have the last say. So she let her have it—the last say. "Have you got any plans for today?" Kate bit down on her upper lip and exhaled through her nose.

Helen shrugged and sipped her coffee. "The washing needs to be done, so I'm going to take care of that today."

Helen liked to do laundry—a lot of it. Though Kate couldn't understand it, she let Helen get on with it. It was one less thing for her to worry about. Her mother ran the machine every single day.

"Oh, and Evan is coming over for dinner tonight. I forgot to tell you." Helen said it like it was the most normal thing in the world.

Kate looked up from her cup of tea, her annoyance undisguised. "What do you mean you forgot to tell me? When was this planned?"

"I asked him to come by when he dropped Adam back off yesterday."

Evan spent weekends with Adam whenever he could. He'd come for him in the morning and return in the early afternoon.

"Okay, fine, but why? And why would you do so without telling me?"

"Do I need a reason to invite my son-in-law to dinner?"

Kate rubbed her nose and kept her eyes on the table. She counted to three in her head—one, two, three, breathe. "Not this again, Ma, please! We're divorced—remember? He's no longer my husband and surprise, surprise...also no longer your son-in-law!"

"Do not use that tone with me. I can hear you well enough with you shouting," Helen raised her chin. "It's not the way I see it. He's my grandson's father, therefore he is my son-in-law."

Kate pursed her lips. "Mark is coming over for dinner. What am I gonna do now?"

"Oh, but you didn't care to tell me that?"

"What? Why—"

"Why would you tell me?" Helen completed her sentence for her. "Don't I live here too? Don't I deserve the same re-spect?"

"You know, what? Fine. Forget I said anything." There was no use arguing. Her mother always won. Rather, Kate always let her mother win. Respect was a big thing in Helen's eyes and sometimes, the fights just weren't worth the trouble that came with it. "I have to do a quick grocery shop," she said. "Do you want to come along or will you stay home with Adam?" Kate's voice was flat.

"We'll stay home," Helen said, clearly content with her win.

Fine. Kate was secretly grateful. She needed some time alone. It had been a while since she'd had a moment to just ap-preciate her own company. The grocery store was as a good as an afternoon in a spa getting a massage. She'd take that as her win. "Is there anything specific you want for tonight?" she asked, regretting the question as soon as it came out.

Helen smiled broadly. "How about we have some *lengua*?" she suggested.

"You want me to get some ox tongue?" Kate wrinkled her nose. "That's going to take hours to cook. And I don't even know where to get that. Besides, I don't think either Mark or Evan are going to enjoy that." Unbelievable.

"You asked me and that was my suggestion." Helen set Adam down in his highchair. "Your father used to make it for me all the time."

Your father this, your father that. Kate couldn't take any more of it. "You forget—I'm not my father." There! She'd said it. And just as Helen opened her mouth to say something, Kate added, "Never mind, I'll go and see what I can get. We'll make a simple dinner. Nothing too onerous." Kate grabbed her purse and gave Adam a kiss on the cheek. "I'll see you soon, my lovey. Be good for Lola."

"About that," Helen said.

What is this time? Kate thought to herself. She closed her eyes and clenched her jaw tight.

"I think I'd like Adam to call me something else."

"Like what?" Kate's chest was burning; it was going to explode.

"Well, Lola makes me sound so old," she said.

"It makes you sound as if you're his grandmother, which—I hate to break it to you—you are."

"Why do you have to be so sarcastic all the time?" Helen snapped.

Back off, Kate, she told herself. "Fine, if that's what you want." Kate shifted from one foot to the other. "What do you want him to call you?"

"That wasn't so hard, was it?" Helen beamed. "You love Mommy Helen, don't you, Adam?" she cooed. "How about Mommy Helen?"

"Ma-ma-ma-ma-ma," Adam looked up at his grandma and gurgled sweet nothings. He'd gotten more vocal, and it brought a smile to Kate's face. She loved him like she never knew she could love anyone. But Mommy? Really? She didn't know how she felt about Adam calling his grandmother Mommy.

"What about Nana?" Kate offered.

Helen's smile dropped into a frown. "You know that nana means puss in Filipino, right? That green puss infection?"

"Fine—Gammy?"

Helen laughed and made smacking noises with her gums. "Sounds like gummy. I still have all my teeth."

Kate was losing her patience. "Mimi?"

"No."

"Fine! Mommy Helen." Kate turned and walked out of the house. Once outside, she took a deep breath in and slowly exhaled. She hated that she could not stand up to her mother. Hated it.

Chapter 12

Sarah Delaney

It was only the first week back at school and already Sarah had been called in to see Noah's teacher.

"I'm sorry, Mrs. Delaney, but we really do need to talk about Noah's behavior," the teacher had said.

Sarah studied the woman's face. Her feigned empathy was well-rehearsed. It was perfect. Sarah wondered how many times she'd had this conversation with other parents before.

What could she say? Sarah had agreed to take Noah to see a specialist. The prospect frightened her. But as Louise had said, "To not take him would be a disservice to him. And besides, you're only doing what's best for him. They're there to help him—and you."

Sarah glanced around the room as she waited for Noah's name to be called. There were others around. Mothers and sons, mothers and daughters. There were fathers, too. All of them, parents waiting to learn the fates of their children as decided by specialists.

"First time?" The mother next to her asked.

Sarah nodded. She wasn't in the mood for any conversation.

"It's always difficult the first time," the woman said. "Don't worry," she smiled gently.

Don't worry. But Sarah was worried. How could she not be? She cast a glance at Noah. To those that didn't know him, Noah looked like a normal little boy. His curly blond hair fell just slightly over his big blue eyes. "Mommy, look at this,"—he said, holding up a toy for her to see—"it's a fire truck!"

Sarah smiled at Noah as if he'd just successfully uncovered an ancient artifact. If there was anything wrong with him—

"Mrs. Delaney?"

Sarah's thoughts were interrupted. She looked up to see a young woman—likely in her mid-twenties; no more than thirty-years-old. Almost immediately, panic rose within her and her palms began to sweat. Her son was going to be in the hands of an infant.

"Noah," she called to him as he busied himself with the toys in the waiting room. "The doctor is ready for us."

She should have thought this through ahead of time. It wasn't unusual for him to ignore her when he was engrossed in an activity. "Noah," she called again. Turning to the young doctor, she said, "I'm sorry, he's been waiting a while."

Sarah went to where Noah played and took him gently by the arm. "Let's go, Noah, it's our turn now."

Noah yanked his arm away from her. "But I'm still playing." Noah turned back to the toys; his legs sprawled across the mat.

"That's enough now." Sarah took the fire truck from him and the moment that she did, she regretted it.

Noah let out a cry and jumped up as he tried to reach for the truck in Sarah's hand.

"I said, that's enough," she said sternly. "You're not listening to me." Speaking calmly to Noah had never really helped in the past, and she didn't know why she thought it would work this time. Noah threw himself on the floor, kicking and screaming.

Blood rose to Sarah's cheeks as the heat spread across to her ears. She could feel the eyes of everyone in the waiting room on her—judging her. Sarah grabbed Noah's arm and lifted him up as he kicked and screamed. Carrying him, she followed the doctor into the office.

THAT NIGHT, AFTER SHE'D put the children to bed, Sarah sat in the living room with Caleb. She stared at the rug underneath her feet.

"Do you wanna talk about what happened?" Caleb asked her. "What did the doctor say?"

Sarah's curled her legs underneath her. She bit on her thumbnail. "They think he might have ADHD."

Caleb nodded slowly. "Attention deficit—"

"Hyperactivity disorder." She'd said the words in her head several times that day. Attention deficit hyperactivity disorder. There was a time when she thought it was one of those made up labels given to children who misbehaved—spoiled kids, those who refused to listen to their parents. But now, she wasn't so sure.

"Okay—well, that's something we can work with. Is it definite?"

Caleb was calm. He was always so calm and cool. It was probably why they made a great couple. But this time, his calmness annoyed Sarah. She shook her head and sniffed in irritation. "We're going to have to go to a few more follow-up sessions before they make a decision." She was afraid for Noah and the life ahead of him. "What's gonna happen to him?" she asked softly, as she allowed the tears she'd held in all day to flow.

Caleb took her hand in his. "Lots of kids have ADHD. It's not a big deal—"

"Not a big deal?" Sarah glared at him. "How can you say that?" Sarah was beside herself. "It's why he can't get through school without an incident happening. It's why he hasn't started reading yet. Or why he can't concentrate on anything. He doesn't know how to share. He can't control his temper. The children don't like him; so yes, Caleb—it is a big deal!"

Caleb sighed. "What I mean is that it's not as uncommon as you might think. There are medications for that sort of thing and—"

"I don't want him to go on medication! What will that do to him?" Thoughts raced around Sarah's head as quickly as her heart banged against her chest. "And Helen—she's going to gloat that she was right; that there is something wrong with my son!"

"Who cares what Helen says?" Caleb got up from the sofa and paced the room. "This isn't about her! You're letting your thoughts overwhelm you. This has absolutely nothing to do with Helen."

Caleb was right, and Sarah knew as much. She was embarrassed for even thinking it. She smoothed the furrow between her eyebrows. "You're right. I'm just being stupid."

Caleb sat down next to Sarah on the sofa. He put his arm around her and pulled her close. "We'll get through this, okay? We'll get through this together."

Sarah leaned into Caleb's embrace. Will we? Sarah thought as her mind traveled back to when she was ten-years-old, maybe eleven.

"Leo, get down here!" her foster dad yelled at the bottom of the steps.

Leo was hiding under Sarah's bed. She could feel his fear; she could hear it in his breathing. "Don't tell him I'm here, Sarah, please don't tell him."

"Where is he?" Mr. Hart was a large man. He was also very tall that his head was nearly as high as the door frame. It wasn't easy to lie to someone like him.

Sarah didn't like living with the Harts. Every day was a battle. The yelling, the cries, the screams. She didn't like it. But she had no choice. No one ever listened to the children.

Leo had ADHD, and he was always getting into trouble—at school, at home. Sarah couldn't bear to hear his cries every time Mr. Hart struck him, which mostly was every day.

He eventually found Leo, and they were both punished, beaten with a belt and anything else he could get his hands on.

Sarah cried quietly into her pillow that night and prayed to God, begging him to hear her. Please, God, please make it all stop. Please make him stop hurting Leo and me.

The next morning, Leo was gone. He'd been sent back. Sarah didn't get to see him go. She didn't get to say goodbye.

Sarah didn't know who of them was the lucky one—her...or Leo.

Sarah leaned into Caleb, comforted by his touch. She was grateful for his tender presence; to know she had someone on her side—looking after her, caring for the children. She would never let anyone else raise her children. Not the Johnsons or the Harts. Never.

She closed her eyes and inhaled his scent. Sarah could feel the screams inside her rising, bellowing, begging to be released. Tears seeped through the corners of her closed eyes. Why did everything have to be so hard?

Chapter 13

Louise Delaney

Things were not going well for Louise. So far, she'd forgotten two sales meetings, and she'd turned up a day early for an appointment with the bank manager. It was disconcerting and, quite frankly, frightening.

On Wednesday morning, Louise sat across from George, the nurse practitioner. It was just as she'd done six months before, and another six months before that.

The last two years had been laden with visits to the specialist. They'd poked, prodded, and conducted tests on her to try to work out why she'd been feeling so off kilter. She was relieved when her blood tests came back perfectly normal. And when the same was said of her brain scan, she was elated. Apart from what the doctor referred to as normal shrinkage, everything was normal. What Louise hadn't expected to fail was the memory test. Apple, eggs, chair. It was those darned words that had tripped her up.

"Okay, Louise," George said, "today we're going to do just a really quick and easy memory test. Is that alright with you? Just like we did the last time you were here."

Louise nodded. "Certainly." His nasally voice annoyed her. She looked at George, his black-framed glasses hanging over the bridge of his nose. Perhaps it was his glasses. Maybe they pinched his nose too much.

"Wonderful. Now, can you tell me what day it is today?"

Louise shifted in her seat and crossed her legs. She clasped her hands and cleared her throat. "Wednesday."

"Very good," he said. "And where are we right now?"

"The clinic." Louise bit down on her upper lip. She hated the questions. They made her feel stupid.

"Well done," George cheered. "What town are we in?"

She hated him. Louise was sure she hated him. "Carlton Bay."

"Very good, Louise. Just super!"

Louise blew throughout her nose and cocked her head to the right. "Do you have to talk to me like I'm stupid?" Louise wasn't normally confrontational, but this man was asking for it.

"Let's move on," the nurse said. "I'm going to tell you names of three things and I want you to repeat those words back to me, okay?" He widened his eyes and spoke as if he were a preschool teacher. "Apple, eggs, chair. Now, it's your turn."

Louise glared at him and wondered if leaping across the table and strangling George would land her in the county lock-up. Clicking her tongue, she said, "Apple."

"Good, that's really good," George said. "Can you remember the next one?"

Louise took a deep breath. "Eggs."

"Okay, you're doing really well, Louise."

She wanted to scream at him and tell him to shut up. The worst part was she couldn't tell the girls or laugh about it with them. What was she supposed to say? That she was forgetting things? So what? Everyone forgets things. The only difference was that she was forgetting more and more as the days went by.

"Louise?"

Her eyes flickered back at George, who was waiting, a smile plastered across his face. She narrowed her eyes, focusing on the tip of his nose—blackheads. Louise had the urge to reach over and squeeze them all out. How fulfilling would that be?

"Louise, can you tell me what the last word was?"

The last word. What in the almighty city of Kansas was that darned word? she thought.

"It's okay," he said, interrupting her thoughts. "Just take your time. Apple, eggs, and? Can you remember the last one?"

Louise shushed him. "Can you please,"—she raised a hand. "Just let me think." Apple, eggs...what was next? Her ears began to ring. Apple, eggs...Louise blinked. "Shoes." She nodded. "It's shoes."

George pressed his lips together into a thin line and scribbled something on his pad. "Okay, that was pretty difficult, I know," he said as if consoling her. "Now, imagine that I give you thirty oranges; and I take away three. How many oranges will you have left?"

"Wait—so what it shoes or not?"

"Let's carry on to the next exercise."

Louise sat up, her back straight. "I need to know if the word was shoes."

"It won't be too long now, Louise. Let's keep going," George said. "Again, imagine that I give you thirty oranges; and I take away three. How many oranges will you have left?"

Fine. She preferred talking to Dr. Bloomfield anyway. George was just another thorn in her side. Louise was good at mathematics. She was a businesswoman, and math came easily to her. She opened her mouth, but her mind fogged up. "Thirty oranges, take away three," she repeated the question in her head. Louise frowned. "It's—uh—"

"That's alright, take your time."

"Thirty oranges," Louise said under her breath. "Uhm, it's—" She cursed. "I'm sorry, I'm sorry," she said. "I don't normally curse." She continued the expletives in her head.

"That's okay. Take your time, Louise."

Louise groaned. "Can you please shut that pickled mouth of yours?" she yelled. "I can't think with you telling me to take my time. I can't hear my own self thinking when you're talking to me at the same time, can I?"

George's overly cheerful face fell.

Louise sighed. "I'm sorry," she said as she put a hand to her forehead. "Twenty-seven. The answer is twenty-seven."

Greg scribbled something down again. "I think that's enough for today," he said. "Don't you?" His smile was back and his nose was still too large. "Well done."

BACK HOME, LOUISE GOT off the phone with Sarah, who'd told her about Noah's appointment with the specialist. Darned specialists! While she felt for her friend, she just couldn't be bothered to listen. There was too much going on and she didn't feel like she could take much more. She had her own problems too. That was why when Sarah asked if she wanted to meet for a cup of tea, Louise had politely declined, saying she had a hot bath calling her name. "Sorry, darling," she'd said. "Maybe tomorrow."

It wasn't a lie, though. She had run a bath and was eager to soak in the tub and forget all else, even if only for a moment—the irony of it escaping her. Louise dipped her hand in the water. Abby was out with Shelby and she wasn't due to see Philip until the morning. Perfect, she thought as she took her hand out of the water. The smell of lavender filled the bathroom, and the steam from the hot water comforted her.

Louise stepped out of her robe and hung it on the hook on the wall. Slowly, she raised a leg to get into the tub—but at the last moment, she turned around, remembering that she'd wanted to play some music. The movement, however, had been too quick that when she turned, taking her foot over the tub, Louise felt her ankle twist. She winced in pain and reached for the sink to steady herself. Instead, she lost her balance hitting her forehead and landed on the floor.

Louise let out a small moan before everything went black.

Chapter 14

Abby Delaney

Abby could sense that things were changing. Something wasn't quite right with Louise. For starters, her commitment to the bookstore hadn't been what it used to be. It was as if any enthusiasm she had for Chapter Five had just disappeared. She hardly ever went out anymore and was, at times, on edge.

She didn't want to leave Louise home alone and was just about to bail on Shelby, when Louise insisted she was fine and needed some time to herself. "You go on and have fun," Louise had said to her. "I'm looking forward to just soaking in the bath and doing absolutely nothing."

Abby hesitated, but in the end, she'd agreed when Louise promised that she would call her if there was anything she needed. "We're just going to the movies and grab some pizza for dinner. Do you want anything?" Abby asked.

"No, no...I'll be fine right here. I don't feel like eating," Louise said with a wave of a hand. "In fact, I just might treat myself and open a bottle of wine."

Abby frowned. "But you don't drink."

"I know," Louise laughed, "but sometimes, it just feels nice to hold a glass in your hand."

"Sounds dumb," Abby said.

"What's dumb, my darling girl, is you wasting your time worrying about me," Louise said. "Must I say I need time away from people?"

"That's better than saying you want to open a bottle of wine and pretending you're a drinker," Abby said.

"Okay, fine," Louise said. "I don't want to be around anyone right now. I'd like to enjoy my own company, hear my thoughts, and do whatever I want to do without worrying about anyone else. How's that?"

Abby grinned. "Better—but what are you gonna do?"

"Things people do when they're alone."

"Eew—"

"What? Why?" Louise smiled. "If you get your head out of the gutter, young lady, you'll see there was nothing wrong with what I said."

"Fine."

"Wonderful! Now go, so I can be at peace."

Chapter 15

Kate Morgan

Instead of heading straight to the grocery store, Kate decided to stop into Louise's place for a quick word and to ask if she wanted to join them for dinner. She thought that having Louise there might help to minimize any tension around the table now that both Mark and Evan were going to be there. Louise was always a calming presence. She always knew what to do when things got awkward.

Kate couldn't get over how her mother had gone and invited Evan without her consent. Although she and Evan were coping well with co-parenting, they were still working on being in the same room together, especially when Mark was around. It was Kate's hope that one day, they could be friends. She imagined Evan and Adam doing 'man things' when Adam was older—fishing, hunting, playing ball...those sorts of activities.

She smiled when she crossed the street. Kate loved Mulberry Lane. It was always so quiet and peaceful. The trees that framed their small cul-de-sac were well-established, painting the street with beautiful hues of reds and oranges. Unlike her home in Manila, nature reigned in Carlton Bay. Kate had never been a nature-kind-of-girl, but since moving to the small town, she felt her heart open up for the big skies.

Kate walked up to Louise's front door. She rang the bell and followed with a knock as she stood and waited for Louise to answer; knowing that Abby and Philip were away.

She looked around to check that Louise's car was in the driveway—it was. Once more, Kate knocked on the door.

Kate pulled her phone out of her back pocket, but before she could find Louise's name, she heard a voice calling out.

She took a step back and looked up. The bedroom light was on.

Then she heard it again.

"Louise?" Kate called out as she rang the bell again and knocked with more urgency on the door. She tried the doorknob, but it was locked.

"Help!"

Kate heard it clearer this time. "Louise!" she called out in a panic. She called Louise's phone, but it just kept ringing. Kate slipped the phone back in her pocket and headed straight for the pot where she knew Louise kept a spare key.

"Louise!" Kate pushed the door open. Dim lights dotted the quiet house. "I'm coming up," she called as she ran up the stairs, taking two steps at a time, and headed straight for Louise's bedroom. "Louise?"

"In here," Louise said.

Kate rushed towards the bathroom and opened the door to find Louise lying on the floor. Her leg was twisted and there was blood seeping from a cut on her forehead. "Oh my gosh, are you okay?" Kate grabbed the bathrobe and covered Louise's naked body. She reached for the towel and dabbed the cut on Louise's forehead.

"My leg—it hurts pretty bad." Louise said.

"Can you move?" Kate tried to help her up.

Louise winced and resisted in pain. "I can't—it hurts too much."

"Hang on." Kate pulled her phone out. "I'm calling an ambulance."

Chapter 16

Sarah Delaney

Sarah rushed to the hospital as soon as she heard about Louise's accident. "I'm looking for my friend—Louise Delaney," she said to the receptionist once she arrived. "She was taken here last night by ambulance."

The receptionist typed into her computer and twisted her lips. "Louise Delaney, you said?"

"What? Is she okay? Is something wrong?" Panic filled Sarah's voice.

"No—I'm sorry, dear," the receptionist smiled. "I was just—never mind. Here we go, I've got her. She's in room 1107. Up on the first floor to your left.

"1107—thank you." Sarah hurried towards the elevator and when she saw it was a few floors away, she opted for the stairs.

When she got to room 1107, she knocked on the door and pushed it open. Louise was in bed with Kate sitting by her side. "Are you okay? What happened?" Tears streamed down her face. She wished she didn't weep so easily, but these days, everything made her cry.

"I'm fine," Louise said with a smile. "There's no need for tears." She was groggy, but looked to be in good spirits.

"I don't understand—what happened?" Sarah went to sit on the bed, but thought otherwise when she saw the cast on Louise's leg. "My goodness!"

"It was a freak accident," Louise said.

"Kate said you took a fall—how? What were you doing?"

Louise nodded. "I fell. Lucky for me, Kate just happened to be at the door, coming to visit."

"I thought it was odd that her car was in the driveway, but she wasn't answering the door," Kate said. "And when I phoned her, she didn't pick up either."

"Thank goodness you were there," Sarah said to Kate before turning back to Louise. "I was so worried when Kate phoned me about it. I wish I could have come sooner."

"It's okay, darling," Louise said. "I'm fine. There wasn't much anyone else could do, anyway."

"Have you told Philip?" Sarah asked Kate.

Kate nodded. "He's already here. He's just gone to get some tea."

"And here it is," Philip said with a smile as he walked into the room, handing a cup each to Louise and Kate. "Here,"—he turned to Sarah—"you take mine."

Sarah raised a hand. "Thanks, Philp. I'm fine. You have it."

"Are you sure?" Philip was such a kind man. He was always looking after Louise and had even taken to Abby. "I don't mind at all."

"Yes, absolutely," Sarah said. "How long are you going to be here for?" she asked Louise.

"A couple of days, maybe three," Louise said.

"What? Why?"

Louise glanced at Kate and then back at Sarah. "They just want to do some tests. Make sure I haven't got a concussion—that sort of thing."

"Haven't they done that yet?" Sarah hated hospitals. Every time she set foot in it, there was always bad news that followed.

"They did," Kate answered for Louise, "but they just want to make sure."

"You know how doctors are. They tend to overreact when it comes to the elderly," Louise joked.

"You're hardly in that category," Kate countered.

Sarah frowned. Her eyes darted around the room. "Can I bring you anything from home? Something to make your stay more comfortable? I can go get you some books or magazines. What about your knitting?"

"I'm fine, darling. It's all taken care of. Besides, you've got the children to worry about."

"Caleb has them. And I'm sure he wouldn't mind." Sarah felt helpless. First, there was the death of her husband. That was difficult to overcome. Then, Noah's ADHD, her fight with Helen, and now, her best friend was in the hospital. It was getting to be all too much.

Sarah wished she was stronger; more in control. At that moment, everything felt overwhelming.

Chapter 17

Louise Delaney

What her friends didn't know was that Louise had spent the better part of the last year and a half visiting doctors and specialists; each one prescribing the same diagnosis.

It had been a tough year for her. Louise had noticed the changes in herself. It wasn't just how foggy her head had been—the forgetfulness. There were other things too; like when she'd forgotten to turn the stove off after cooking dinner one night. Losing her glasses wasn't something to worry about—that was a pretty normal occurrence. But that time was different. She'd spent the entire day looking for them—under the couch, in the fridge, in the garden where she had been trimming the roses, and every other place she thought was obvious. It was a laughable moment when Abby had arrived home and pointed out that the glasses were on her head. But Louise knew it inside of her. Something was wrong. Exhaustion and irritability had become her new norm.

In the beginning, none of the doctors took her seriously. They'd asked about menopause, and when she told them she'd already gone through it, they moved on to her lifestyle. Was she busy enough? Was she too busy, perhaps? "Owning and managing a bookstore can be quite challenging," one doctor had said. But it'd never been a problem for Louise. She loved the bookstore and the work that came with it. But lately, keeping track of her responsibilities had become more and more difficult; so much so that she'd fallen behind on paying her bills—not because she didn't have the finances, but because she'd forgotten. So, "take a break,"—they'd told her—"slowing down will be good for you. Perhaps it might be time to consider retirement." But she knew. Louise knew there was more to it. She could feel it. After all, no one knew her better than Louise herself.

For a long time, Louise had been told that she didn't fit the criteria. "Of what?" she would ask. It wasn't until one day, after she'd finally met a specialist who was willing to take her concerns seriously, that things became clearer.

"Have you heard of the term early onset Alzheimer's?" Dr. Bloomfield asked.

"Oh no, no, no—" Louise laughed. "I'm old, but not that old," she said, quickly dismissing the ridiculous insinuation.

Dr. Bloomfield held a face, much like the ones you'd see in the movies, where they're not quite sure you want to hear what they have to say...but they have to tell you anyway. "I want to talk about the tests we had you complete. Do you recall those tests?"

Louise frowned. She found it difficult to mask her rising agitation. "I do," she said pointedly.

Dr. Bloomfield paused and pressed his lips together. "Then you will recall that the first thing we did was to get you to do some lab tests."

"Yes, and they come out perfectly normal."

"That's right. Those tests came back as normal. There were no vitamin deficiencies or other problems that could explain your symptoms, including the memory problems you've been experiencing."

Louise clicked her jaw. Dr. Bloomfield was now talking to her in the same way that the nurse practitioner, George, did. Like she was some stupid child, incapable of understanding anything more complex than a newly learned alphabet.

"The neuro-imaging we did allowed us to get pictures of the tissue in your brain to make sure that you hadn't had a minor stroke that wasn't picked up. But even that was normal. There was some shrinkage noted, but nothing out of the ordinary for your age."

Louise bounced her leg impatiently.

"The memory tests we've been doing—those you've been doing with George—do you remember those?"

Louise glared at him. Of course she remembered them.

When Louise didn't respond, Dr. Bloomfield continued. "That's where we saw you encounter some struggles which were consistent with your own observations." He clasped his hands and leaned forward. "All encompassing, everything combined—your medical history, any past medications you've taken—it looks like your memory loss is pointing to Alzheimer's."

No. No. Louise looked around the room. She felt hot around the collar of her sweater; making it hard to breathe. Dr. Bloomfield's mouth had been moving, but her ears were blocked, just like when one is on a descending plane. Louise poked her right ear, encouraging it to pop.

"Now, let's talk about what that means for you. But before that, do you have any questions for me?" Dr. Bloomfield's face was kind and dared she say it, genuine. It was unlike George's face plastered with a well-practiced smile reserved for old people whose memories were failing; people like Louise.

Questions. Yes, she had questions. She had a turd ton of questions! What were they? "How long does it take—you know—for the...?" What was she trying to say? "You know, the phases; how long..." her voice trailed off, replaced by the tears she'd fought hard to keep at bay.

"I know this is a difficult conversation we're having," Dr. Bloomfield said, passing a box of tissues to Louise.

"Thank you," Louise said. He probably had boxes and boxes in his drawers and cupboards; ready to be passed on at the first sign of weakness. The first sign of tears. How many times had he delivered similar news to his patients? Was it hard for him to do so? Did he take pleasure in delivering such life-changing news?

"By the time a person with Alzheimer's displays symptoms; or starts noticing the changes—research shows that the disease has already been working through the brain for over at least a decade. From that perspective, the progression is at pace. We might even call it slow." Dr. Bloomfield cleared his throat. "But now that we know what we're dealing with, we can be proactive about it. We can talk about some strategies to help you keep living your life as you're used to; strategies to keep you as healthy as we possibly can."

It had hit her like a brick; a kick to the guts. How could that be? What kind of cruel joke was this? Alzheimer's? No. It couldn't be! Good God! Louise was never one to use the Lord's name in vain. But seriously, dear God, seriously. She looked up at the hospital-white ceiling. Why were doctor's office always so white?

"There are some medications that you might wish to consider. There are also a lot of things you can do yourself—socializing, exercising, and generally making sure you're using your brain."

Louise snorted. It began with a sniff, then a chuckle, followed by a row of expletives. But Dr. Bloomfield let her...he let her curse at him, curse at God. And when she'd finished, he continued. "I can connect you with a social worker, one who is well-versed in living with Alzheimer's. Is there anyone in your family who can be part of these meetings? It's always a good idea to have a support person."

Philip. How could she tell Philip? And the others? How was she going to tell the girls? What would she do with the bookstore? And Abby...Abby was still so young. She had her whole life ahead of her, and Louise couldn't bear the thought of leaving her so soon; not when they'd only just found each other.

A few weeks after her diagnosis, it happened. Philip had asked her about her condition. She'd forgotten to meet him at the Italian restaurant on Lighthouse Road. It was supposed to be a romantic dinner, but Louise didn't turn up.

"I just think we need to take caution, Lou. You've been forgetting a lot of things lately. And the falls you've been having—it's dangerous," Philip had said. He stroked his eyebrow. "I think it's time to see a doctor."

So she told him. Louise told him everything that, for months, she'd kept to herself. "I have early onset Alzheimer's," she'd said, her mouth running dry.

Philip froze, blinking slowly. Louise could see he was stunned, much like she'd been when she first found out. He'd tried to hide his shock—bless him—but she could see right through his facade.

They'd talked long into the night that day. Together, holding each other, they sat on the sofa; him making promises of forever, and her reminding him to be realistic.

She would be lying if she said she wasn't angry. Why her? What had she ever done to deserve this? Louise made sure God knew she was angry. In addition to cursing and denouncing him, Louise threw a myriad of questions at God; calling on him to answer her. But he never did.

"Louise?" Kate spoke softly, bringing Louise back to the hospital room where everyone's eyes were on her. "What's going on?" she asked, her eyebrows drawn together.

Kate was so perceptive. She was a sweetheart, and Louise wished nothing but a good, healthy, and happy life for her friend.

"You can tell us," Kate said as she squeezed Louise's arm. "What is it?"

Sarah nodded, clearly holding back her tears. Poor Sarah had always been quick to tears. Her husband's death had made her fragile, and Louise felt protective of her. But she didn't want tears. She'd cried enough. She was tired of crying. Tired of being angry. Tired of asking questions. So for the second time since it had been confirmed, Louise spoke the very words she'd hoped to deny. Her eyes flitted between her two friends. "I have Alzheimer's."

Winter

Cast your burdens upon Me, those who are heavily laden.
Come to Me, all of you who are tired of carrying heavy loads.
For the yoke I will give you is easy, and My burden is light.
Come to Me and I will give you rest.
~Matthew 11:28-30

Chapter 18

Kate Morgan

Winter had come around quickly that year with everyone pretending things were normal, which seemed to be the common theme. Pretense. Falsehoods. Denial.

Kate had found a job as a caregiver working at the same retirement home that Louise's mother had spent the last years of her life. They'd offered her a job providing one-on-one care to a resident named Bruce Lester, an antagonistic ninety-year-old who had lung cancer. Though an unusual set-up, Bruce's care demanded that no 'poking or prodding' take place, and that he was to live the remainder of his life as nature saw fit. Abiding by his wishes, Bruce's family requested that no intervention be carried out when it came to his health. All he required from the retirement village was a place to stay and a companion to see to his needs. In return, his family paid a hefty fee.

Without any health qualifications, Kate had been the perfect candidate. She was chosen for the fact that she wasn't a nurse. Her role focused mainly on making up Bruce's room and helping him with his personal care needs, such as showering and getting dressed. It wasn't in line with her degree in hotel and restaurant management, but the hours were good and it paid the bills.

To Kate, the experience was both dismal and humbling.

When she'd first began working with Bruce, he'd made it clear that he did not like her. He'd wanted "someone white and whose skin color does not resemble dirt and mud", he'd said. "Someone who talks properly, like an intelligent American." Bruce had done everything he could think of to make Kate's job as difficult as possible, and even went as far as soiling his clothes and his bed despite having full control of his bladder and bowel functions.

But she wasn't going to let him put her down as if she was some uncivilized, downtrodden pest. She had enough of that from her mother. "I'm a university graduate, Bruce. I have a degree. My skin is brown and I'm glad I don't have to pay to get a spray tan, because Lord knows I can't deal with any more unnecessary bills. I'm missing my son's many milestones and my best friend is the last chapters of her life and rather than looking after them, I'm stuck here taking care of you. You know why, Bruce? Because I have to. Because that's life. We all gotta things we don't really want to do. I'm all you've got now, and it's gonna be you and me against the world." Kate had said to him. "So I suggest you get used to it and start treating me kindly, with even just a smidge of respect, if you can manage it, because we're going to be spending lots of time together," she said. "Or you can go and find yourself another caregiver."

Kate didn't know how she'd managed to get that all across to him, but from that day onwards, Bruce had become kinder to Kate; sometimes even cracking a joke or two.

Another part of the job that she hadn't fully expected was to see the goings on in the dementia ward. Whilst she didn't directly work with the patients with dementia, she could see how the disease took over each of those who themselves once were nurses, teachers, mothers, and fathers.

"It's terrible, isn't it?" Bruce had said to her one afternoon as they rested on a bench underneath a large mulberry tree. The retirement village sat isolated at the end of town, surrounded by sprawling gardens and places where residents and patients could take part in gentle activities; providing them with a sense of normality. "One minute you're celebrating the highs of life, feeling like you're on top of the world—unstoppable, uncaring, fearless." Bruce coughed into his fist. "The next minute, you're in this place and someone is feeding you with a teaspoon and wiping the drool off your chin. It's a travesty. A mockery of humanity, if you ask me."

Kate feared for Louise and what lay ahead of her. She couldn't understand how someone so young and so healthy could be ridden with such an aggressive disease.

Since Louise's accident, they moved their Tea for Three get-togethers to Louise's house. It made it easier, especially as Louise still had a cast on her leg and was likely to have it on for the next while. Her doctor had said they were looking at twelve weeks. Catching up at her place also gave Kate and Sarah a chance to weed the garden and keep it in shape while Louise was unable to. They knew how much Louise loved her garden and wanted to help make things easier for her.

"How are things going with Helen?" Louise asked Kate, who was down on her knees pulling out a nasty weed.

"About as impossible as this weed," Kate said, giving it one more tug. "Ah-ha! I did it!" she said, beaming.

"Darling, I honestly don't understand why you let her walk all over you," Louise said as she sat on the garden chair with her leg perched up on a footstool.

Sarah joined them from the kitchen with a tray of tea and cookies. "Come and take a break, Kate," Sarah said. "I've made us a fresh pot."

Kate pushed herself up from the ground and dusted her knees. She took her garden gloves off and dropped it next to the weeding fork.

"Now, tell me," Louise said, raising the subject again. "Why do you let her act the way she does?"

Kate sighed. "She's my mom."

"And?" Louise took her sunglasses off and rested it on her head.

"I've actually been wondering the same for some time now," Sarah agreed.

"Well, and there's you too, you know," Louise nodded towards Sarah.

"Me?" Sarah asked in surprise.

"Yes, you," Louise raised her eyebrows.

Kate was glad for the attention to be off her.

"Both of you," Louise said. "Shall we pour the tea?"

"I'll do it," Sarah said. "What about me?"

"Now, Kate, darling—you know I love you dearly, but I have to say that I am hugely disappointed in how you let your mother get away with so much," Louise continued.

Kate frowned. She'd agonized over her mother for months, but she always ended up in the same dinghy of uncertainty. She had no idea what to do or how to handle their worsening situation. It felt like she was floating aimlessly, no oars or paddles to row with.

"And Sarah," Louise turned to her. "I can see you tip-toeing over this whole thing with Noah. So he has ADHD—so what? Darling, there's so much more in the world that can go wrong. ADHD can be managed and you need to start propping him up so that he can be the best young man he was meant to be. Get him the treatment he needs and stop hiding him away from people. It's time you allowed him to attend birthday parties again. Keeping him at home just so that he doesn't throw a potential tantrum is just ridiculous. You can't keep doing that to him or yourself. And what about poor Caleb? What kind of time does he have with you?"

Sarah's face reddened. "But—"

Louise waved a hand in the air as if waving a fly. "Now, I have kept my mouth zipped for months now. I've waited for you both to step up, but neither of you have and this has to stop."

Kate narrowed her eyes at Louise. "Look, you don't understand," Kate said in a bid to defend herself. "I have to make sure she's happy. She's alone now, and I'm all she's got."

"Darling, if your mother continues the way she's been carrying on, it may serve well to lose you—then she'll really be alone. She is your mother, not your master." Louise was adamant and carried on. "Kate, you, my girl—you know I love you and I know you might think I'm being harsh—but you need to grow a backbone. You stood up to Evan when he was mistreating you, so why are you allowing Helen to do the same? She will continue to use and abuse you for as long as you let her. People will treat you the way you allow them to treat you. This is your life and if you don't live it for yourself, then someone else will."

"Why are you doing this?" Sarah asked on the verge of tears.

"Because one day, I will forget to tell you," Louise said. "And then it will be too late."

Uncertain, Kate's mouth broke into a smile. "Are you seriously pulling the A-card?"

"Alzheimer's,"—Louise said—"say it with me. Alzheimer's."

Kate flinched. "No."

"We've got to accept this if we're going to be in it together," Louise said.

"Fine—Alzheimer's," Kate said out loud.

"Alzheimer's," Sarah followed with a smile.

"I will not let this disease beat me," Louise said. "Not yet! For now, it's simply a nuisance." Louise took a sip of her tea.

Kate wanted to cry. Her lips trembled. She wanted to leave, to run away from it all.

"Uh-uh,"—Louise wagged a finger at her—"no tears, my darling. Back straight, keep your chin up, don't let the world see you cry." She turned to Sarah. "Especially you, Sarah. I love you, but my darling, you've got to stop crying every time something goes wrong. And when the day comes that I forget to tell you, I want you both to remember and remind each other. You hear me?"

Kate heard her, loud and clear. Her heart swelled with pride for best friend. Among the three of them, Louise had all the reasons to give up. But she refused to. She was strong and determined; simply amazing. Kate hoped that one day, she too could be strong.

"I think I need some chocolate," Louise said with a sly smile.

"Me too," Kate laughed.

"Make that three," Sarah added.

UNFORTUNATELY FOR KATE, it was easier said than done. Once back home, Kate found herself bound by cultural traditions and firmly held values. There was nothing Kate could do but to serve her mother's wants and whims. Kate had been taught that her mother was and would always be the queen of the house. "There can only be one queen," she'd told Kate, growing up. "Men go on to serve their wives and, by default, their mothers-in-law. But daughters are the ones who will stick by you and care for their parents as they move into old age." It had been Helen's way of telling Kate where her place was. Following blindly, eager to please her mother, Kate submitted and kept to that place.

She had always put her family first. She aimed to please her parents at every turn. So when Kate fell in love with Evan and left for the United States, she knew she'd failed as a daughter. But now, she'd been given another chance to serve her mother; a chance to make up for what she'd done wrong. And so, once again, Kate did as her mother pleased, as such was the imperative of her psychological conditioning.

Working at the retirement village had given Kate the much-needed room to breathe. Space and time away from her mother; space and time to be herself.

Things had come to a head when one day, when Kate had returned home and found that Helen had shaved off all of Adam's hair. "What have you done?" she'd cried.

"I don't see why you're so upset, Kate," Helen had argued. "It was always going to happen, and it was long overdue. You knew that!"

"But I wanted to be the one to do it." She knew it was what they'd traditionally done, and it was what she had intended to do. But after the death of her father and then making room for her mother to move in, the tradition had fallen by the wayside. "Did you not think that I'd want to be here when it happened?"

"Oh, stop being so dramatic." Helen pulled out an envelope containing the first of Adam's cut locks—the one that should have been snipped by Sarah and Louise, and stuffed into a book.

She took the envelope and held the soft curly lock of hair in her hands. Kate picked Adam up, running her hand over his hairless head. A pinch of sadness overwhelmed her. "Did he cry?"

"Obviously." Helen looked at Kate as if surprised that she'd even asked the question. "He's a baby. That's what they do."

"Well, I'd cry too if someone held me down and shaved my hair off," Kate mumbled.

"What?" Helen asked pointedly, clearly irritated. "Stop mumbling, Kate. You're not a child."

"Exactly! I'm an adult and you need to start treating me like one," she cried.

Helen glared at Kate; her face, tight. "Maybe I will when you start acting like one."

Kate flinched, and her pulse quickened. There was something about Helen—something about how she acted, the words she spoke—that always made Kate retreat and withdraw to the days back when she was a teenager. She was afraid to disappoint her mother and had only ever wanted to please her. "Why can't I ever please you?" she shouted and threw her hands up.

Helen frowned. "Me? Why do you need to please me?"

"All I ever wanted was to please you. But it seems that no matter what I do, I always get it wrong. It's never enough for you." Kate's throat tightened up, her jaw hurting as she clenched her teeth. She tried to hold her tears back, but they pushed past her eyelids. "It will never be enough for you, will it? Nothing I do will ever be enough for you!"

"Oh, please," Helen rolled her eyes and sneered. "Stop with the theatrics. Don't do things for others, especially if it affects your own life. Do things only if you really want to. You don't have to please me. You can tell me to back off. In fact, you should tell me to back off. Don't give me the power to control your life. I have no wish to control anybody."

It made perfect sense to Kate. Every single word. You can tell me to back off. In fact, you should tell me to back off. But why couldn't she bring herself to do it? Just like that, Kate's heart crumbled. Again. Just like the many times in the past. She knew that she needed to overcome the control that her mother had over her. She knew she needed to grow up. But whenever a moment arose, she backed down. It was the same way that she'd back down whenever her Evan lost his temper. Maybe her mother was right. Maybe the problem was with Kate.

"Let's stop this, Katherine," Helen said, her voice soft and in control. "Your father wouldn't be happy about it."

Kate fell quiet—just as she always did. She was ashamed of herself and her inability to stand up to her mother. She backed away from Helen, widening the physical distance between them, and headed up to her bedroom, which had become her only place of solace.

She sent a text message to Mark telling him not to come that night, but he wasn't happy about it. She scoffed at the irony of it—both her mother and her boyfriend were mad at her. She climbed into bed and closed her eyes.

In that moment, Kate's whole life felt like a prison.

As Kate lay in bed, she stared up at the ceiling. "Where are you?" she asked God. "Why is this happening?" Tears fell from her eyes and gathered in her ears. It had been a while since she'd talked to God; but now, more than ever, she needed to feel his presence. Kate got up and grabbed her guitar from the closet.

The guitar was out of tune, just like her life. Kate hummed a key and plucked each string until the notes sounded just right.

Eyes closed, Kate breathed in deeply. She plucked at the strings and played several chords as she searched for a tune. F-G-C...F-G-C. Her unpracticed fingertips stung as she pressed down on the steel strings of the guitar. And when she finally heard a melody that sounded like the song in her heart, Kate sang the words she'd been holding on to; her prayer to the Lord.

"Hello? Is anyone home today?

I seem to, I maybe have lost my way.

Do you think you can come out and show me how?

The right direction, the way."

Kate sang softly, slowly, finding the words and letting them spill from her heart. She used to write songs—once upon a time, not so long ago. She had dreams of being a stage singer. "Don't hold your breath," her mother had once told her. She was sixteen; maybe seventeen at the time. "I'm the only one who will tell you the truth. Don't listen to people who tell you that you have a nice voice. If you have it, you have it. You—don't." And just like that, any light she had in her heart for singing was snuffed out.

"I know, things aren't going right.

I think I've done everything; I've tried.

I don't know what's going wrong, do you see?

Lord, lead me to the light."

Kate felt her tears gather behind her closed eyes, but she dared not open them. Not now. Not when she was finally talking to God. There was a sweet yodel in her voice; one that only came out when she sang from the heart. Her mother's voice rang in her head. "Why do you sing it like that? It's too sweet. You need to put more raw emotion into it. Like this..." Helen used to tell her, before belting into song; her preferred repertoire.

"Do you think you can come out and show me how?

The right direction, the way.

Lord, lead me to the light.

The right direction...the way..."

Kate slumped over her guitar and let her tears flow, as she recalled a verse in the Bible from her days in school. "Cast your burdens upon Me, those who are heavily laden. Come to Me, all of you who are tired of carrying heavy loads. For the yoke I will give you is easy, and My burden is light. Come to Me and I will give you rest."

Kate put a hand over stomach and wept; lost and conflicted.

Chapter 19

Louise Delaney

The next morning, Louise pushed herself up from the sofa and winced as she reached for her crutches. Abby had left early to open the bookstore. It had been a while since Louise had been into work, and had it not been for Abby, she didn't know how she would have managed.

She slowly made her way to the kitchen. It was the first time in her life that she'd ever been in crutches, and she had no idea it would be so difficult to carry her own weight around. She'd taken to sleeping in the living room to save herself the taxing hike up to her bedroom.

Louise looked around the kitchen and tried to recall why she'd gotten up. Her eyes darted around the room—from the fridge to the stove, the dining table to the kitchen counter. *What was it I wanted?* she thought.

The harder she tried, the harder it was to remember. Louise took a deep breath in. Everything looked unfamiliar to her. *Where am I?* She had a sinking feeling in her stomach and her heart pounded against her chest. Dread creeped within her and she began to fret.

The phone rang and startled Louise, bringing her back to her senses. She walked towards the telephone that sat on the left-hand side of the counter. It rang four more times before she picked it up. Gripping the phone with two hands, Louise whispered into the mouthpiece. "Hello?"

"It's me." It was a man. "How are you feeling this morning?"

The voice sounded familiar, but she wasn't sure who it was.

"Lou? Are you there?"

Lou—the only person that ever called her Lou was a boy she'd had a crush on when she was in her teens. She hesitated. "Philip?"

"Yes, it's me. I was just calling to check on how you're doing. Do you want me to come over?"

Louise hadn't heard from Philip since the day she married Warren over forty years ago. He was their wedding celebrant. "Here?" she asked as she looked around. "You want to come here?"

"Lou, is everything okay?"

No, she'd wanted to say. Nothing was okay. Where was she and why was he calling her after all these years?

"I'll be right over," Philip said and hung up.

Louise stared at the phone in her hand. She couldn't see Philip. Not now—not after all the years that have passed between them.

Chapter 20

Kate Morgan

Kate shut the door behind her and walked down the driveway. She needed some air, some time away from her mother. She had few hours before her shift and thought a walk might do her some good.

The sky was much brighter than how she was feeling that morning. As she looked up, Kate rolled her head around, placing a hand behind her neck and gently pressed down. She wondered how much a massage would set her back.

Out of the corner of her eye, Kate saw Louise hobbling quickly towards her.

"Kate!" Louise whispered aloud and looking behind her.

It wasn't like Louise to scurry. "Is everything okay?" Kate asked, thinking something might have happened.

"You have to help me," Louise said, now standing next to Kate.

"What's the matter?" Kate looked around for any sign of danger.

"There's someone coming for me; a man." Louise glanced around again, her eyes flickering, darting back and forth. "He said he's coming." She clutched Kate's arm. "You have to help me."

Kate could feel Louise's fingernails digging into her skin. "Who's coming?"

"I don't know! But he said he's coming!" Fear and panic dotted her face.

"Do you mean Philip?"

Louise stopped; her face drained of all color. "You know him? You know Philip?"

"Of course—"

"But..." Louise's voice trailed off. "I haven't seen him in years—decades! How could you..."

It was the first real sign of the disease that Kate had seen since the diagnosis. Her chest tightened. "Louise, honey, you know Philip," she said, putting her arm around Louise's shoulders, guiding her back towards her house. "He's your partner, remember?" Remember...Kate winced at the word. It was something that her friend, one day soon, would not be able to do.

Louise was visibly shaken. "Yes," she said, her voice shaking. "You're right. Absolutely. Oh gosh, I'm sorry, Kate. I don't know what came over me."

And just like that, the Louise that she knew was back in the present. "I know," Kate comforted her. "We all have those days. Now, let's get you back home. I'll come stay with you for a while, okay?"

Louise had tried to laugh it off, but Kate could tell that she knew it too. They both knew that moment had marked the true beginning of the Alzheimer's taking over. As she walked Louise back to her house, Kate held on to her, never wanting to let go.

She wondered how long it would be before the disease erased any memory of Kate too.

Kate was closest to Louise. She might even go as far as saying that Louise was like a mother to her. Kate couldn't bear the thought of losing Louise.

Chapter 21

Sarah Gardner

Through the living room window, Sarah saw Louise and Kate across the street. She wondered what they were up to and normally, she would have gone to have a quick chat. But things were far from normal in Sarah's household. Between what was happening with Noah and Louise, it was just too much for her.

As the days went by, Sarah found it more and more difficult to connect with Noah; to understand what his triggers were and why he was so different from his siblings. Every day was a struggle. Once again, she found herself overwhelmed by almost everything. Unable to focus, she felt inept at life, as if she'd dropped the ball somehow.

She'd kept Noah home from school for the day to give herself some time to think of what to do. Getting a call or a note from the school every single day wasn't fun, and she didn't like feeling like she was being judged. Maybe they were right to judge her. As it was, Sarah already blamed herself. She'd had depression. It was very likely in her genes. She'd brought this on. She did this to her own son. In a way, Sarah knew for sure that she was to blame for Noah's condition.

"Things were different with Liam." Sarah brought a shaky hand to her forehead. "I can't keep meeting with his teacher about the same thing over and over again. I can feel her judging me each time we meet, as if she's wondering why I've not managed to sort Noah out."

"Don't compare him to Liam and Zoe," Caleb said, as he got ready to leave for work. "It's not fair to Noah—or to any of them. And who cares what they think?"

Sarah crossed her arms and stared out the window. "You don't understand. None of you do." She wanted to cry, but Louise's voice rang in her mind. "Don't you cry, my darling. Back straight, keep your chin up, don't let the world see you cry. I love you, but my darling, you've got to stop crying every time something goes wrong." But Louise didn't understand, Sarah thought. She couldn't possibly. It wasn't her son that was diagnosed with a mental illness.

"Sarah, I'm right here. And I don't need to tell you that I understand your concerns. We're in this together."

"You always say that," she said absentmindedly, "but when it all hits the fan, you'll be straight out the door."

"Really, Sarah?"

Sarah touched a finger to her lips. The words just slipped out of her mouth without her meaning to let them out. She dared not look at Caleb.

"Is that really what you think of me?" Caleb pressed.

"Look, just forget I said anything." From where she stood, it looked like Kate was comforting Louise. Sarah wondered what was going on. A part of her wanted to go and check on her, but the other part was consumed with what was going on with her own family. Noah was still asleep. She didn't wake him when she got the other two ready for school. It wouldn't be long before the quiet house turned into a chaotic space filled with screams, tears, and tantrums. And besides, Louise was just going to tell her to stop worrying so much. She didn't feel like being judged by anyone.

Caleb put his duffle bag down. "No—I think we need to talk about this."

Sarah sighed and rubbed the back of her neck. She didn't want to talk about it. "You're going to be late for work."

"Forget work," he snapped. "Is that really what you think of me?"

Sarah turned and glared at him. "I said I don't want to talk about it, Caleb. You and I both know it. He's not your real son. It'll be easy for you to walk away when things get too hard."

"Are you for real?" Caleb's face was a contortion of hurt and anger. "Are you f—" Caleb shook his head. "You can't be serious." He rubbed his chin. "That was below the belt and you know it," he said, pointing an accusatory finger at her.

She knew she'd hurt him. Sarah could see the veins on his temples pulsing. But it was too late to take any of it back.

"So because I'm not his real dad—nothing I feel can be real. Is that right? Have I not proven enough to you? How much more proof do you need from me, Sarah? Oh wait—it's because I'm not Adam, right?" Caleb walked up to Sarah, prompting her to take a step back. "Because Adam was so darned perfect and no one could possibly measure up to him!"

She wished she could take it all back, but something inside her just pushed and pushed. "It's not the same," she said through gritted teeth.

"What's not the same?" Caleb rubbed his forehead and sighed. He reached for her hand, which she'd instinctively pulled away. "Sarah...talk to me," he said, his voice gentler.

Sarah could feel her eyes begin to sting. She loathed herself for not able to control her feelings. And she hated that Louise was right about her. "Just go, Caleb. I'll be fine. I'm just being overly sensitive," she said. "My period must be coming soon or something." Her period. That would shut him up.

"Sarah—"

"Please—Caleb, please go. I need a moment. I'm sorry for what I said. I'm..." Sarah couldn't finish her sentence. "I just want to be alone for a while."

"Okay, but we're not done here," he said. "We'll talk more about it tonight."

Sarah wasn't a talker. Not when things were falling apart. As far as she was concerned, there was no time for talking. She needed a plan. Adam was good at making plans. He always came up with solutions, things to do, places to go. "Fine," she said.

Caleb kissed her on the cheek. "Everything's going to be fine, you hear? Look at me." He smoothed her chin and caught her eyes with his. "Everything is going to be fine. I promise you."

She wished she could believe him. But Adam's death had left her jaded. How could she not be jaded? They were supposed to grow old together. They'd made their vows—in front of God. For better or worse, in sickness and in health, until death do us part. He was her rock, and her rock had turned to dust.

Death. Yes, it was death that had finally parted them. She'd been angry with God, and she questioned him—challenged him, even. But he never answered. Or maybe had had. He'd sent her Caleb, didn't he?

Troubled thoughts filled her head. Her mind was in a constant tug-of-war, and she felt herself slipping back into the dark well of depression. She'd lifted the well cover and had fallen in.

It was the same feeling she'd had after Adam died. A heavy blanket lay over, suffocating her. She couldn't breathe.

Caleb's voice broke through her thoughts. "You try to have a good day, okay?"

Sarah nodded.

"Don't think too much."

Caleb knew her well. There was no hiding from it. She wasn't a big talker, but she was a deep thinker. And that wasn't always good for her. For Sarah, ruminating was akin to digging her own grave.

Caleb kissed her once more, leaving Sarah still standing by the window. Kate and Louise were no longer in sight, and dangerous as it was, Sarah was again, alone with her thoughts.

Chapter 22

Kate Morgan

Kate nodded and promised Louise that she would not tell anyone about her moment of disorientation. It was a gentle word, disorientation. A gentle way of saying of paranoia...or worse, Alzheimer's.

"It was just a brief moment and I think it would be best if we just don't mention it to anyone else," Louise said. She looked completely in control of her senses; nothing like she was just a few minutes earlier. Louise took her place next to Kate at the kitchen table, handing her a cup of tea.

"Don't you think we should at least tell Philip?" Kate was certain that Philip would want to know.

Louise dismissed the suggestion. "There's no need to alarm him—or anyone else, for that matter." She took the tea bag by the string and wrapped it around the teaspoon, squeezing the remaining liquid. She put the tea bag on an empty saucer before giving her tea a stir and taking a cautious sip.

Kate understood why she wanted it kept from anyone else. The decline was happening all too quickly. Tears welled up in her eyes. "But—"

Louise took Kate's hand. "I don't want to waste time on any tears, so you can quickly wipe those off your sweet face, young lady." And there it was—the Louise that Kate knew so well and loved to no end.

Kate smiled and wiped her tears. "I keep wishing this is all a bad dream. That none of it is real."

"I know," Louise smiled. "Me too. But these things happen and I don't make the rules."

"I'm just so—so angry!" Kate hadn't meant to unburden her feelings. Not right then. And certainly not to Louise. But things were frightening. "I feel like it's all moving too fast.

"God has a plan, darling," Louise said. "He always has a plan."

The mention of God angered her—more than she ever thought possible. Kate had always been a believer. Her faith was strong and not once had she questioned God. But now...this time, things were different. She'd broken that darned mirror, and now everything else around her was breaking into millions of pieces. Her father was gone. Her mother had turned into someone she no longer knew. Noah's ADHD diagnosis was destroying Sarah. And now, Louise. "He's got a plan, huh?" Her tone was stronger than she'd expected, but she couldn't keep it in any longer. "What kind of God would do this to you?" She shook her head. "What kind of God would do this to us?"

"Kate, honey, it's not a big deal. This is life."

"It's a massive deal!" Kate said, her eyes rapidly blinking. It both puzzled and irked her that Louise was so calm. How could she be so calm at a time like this? "I can't"—she stammered—"I can't lose you, Louise."

Louise reached for her hand. "You're not going to lose me."

Kate began to weep. "Why is this all happening? I don't understand..." her voice trailed off.

"You know what they say...God works in mysterious ways. We don't always know what his plans are, but we have to trust in him."

Louise was like a mother to her. When Kate's marriage to Evan failed and he'd sent her away with nowhere to turn to, it was Louise that took her in. And when she'd given birth to Adam without even an inkling of what to do, it was Louise that showed her the ropes. It was Louise who had stayed up late with her on nights when Adam wouldn't sleep; she'd fed him, changed him, and sang to him when Kate needed rest. Louise helped her to believe in herself. "I don't know what I'd do without you..."

"I'm not going anywhere," Louise said. "Not yet, at least. You can't be rid of me that easily. All you need to do is wave a chocolate bar under my nose and I guarantee you I'll come back to my senses."

Kate laughed. Her nose was clogged, and her eyes were puffy, but she was grateful for the release.

"Knock, knock," Philip said as he stood by the kitchen doorway. "The front door was unlocked."

Kate quickly wiped her tears and got up. "Philip," she said, "hi." She glanced at Louise to make sure she was okay.

"Hello darling," Louise smiled. "We were just talking," she said to Philip. "Would you like a cup of tea?"

Philip walked over to where Louise sat and dropped a kiss on her cheek. "How are you feeling?"

"Never better," she beamed and smoothed his cheek.

"I should get going," Kate said. "I've got to leave for work soon." Kate looked at Philip. "You take care of her, okay?"

Philip smiled. "You know I will."

She did. She knew that Philip would look after Louise. She said a quick goodbye and headed back to her house.

Kate's mind was full. It wasn't fair. Since working at the retirement village, Kate saw what Alzheimer's and dementia did to those afflicted with it. Louise didn't deserve that. Why would God let her go in such an undignified way?

Chapter 23

Louise Delaney

Philip helped Louise back into the living room and on to the sofa. He'd pulled the ottoman closer so that Louise could both stretch and rest her legs. She was eager to get the cast off, so that she could return to moving around unhindered. "Thank you, darling," she said with a sigh. "That already feels so much better."

"Is everything okay with Kate?" Philip asked as he sat down next to her.

Louise nodded. "Mmm, yes. Well, she's upset, as I'm sure you'd noticed."

"Do you want to talk about it?" Philip was a perceptive man.

"You know how it is," Louise said. "Kate is still quite young. Some things are just a bit harder for her to accept." It broke her heart to see Kate hurting, but there was nothing she could do but to try to placate her.

"Do you want me to have a talk with her?" Philip offered.

Louise smiled at him. A shiver ran down her spine. It was scary to think that just earlier, she'd forgotten him; that he'd

144

ever returned to her. That after all these years, they were finally together. "She'll come to you when she's ready."

Philip nodded. "How are you feeling?"

Louise wanted to tell him the truth. She wanted to tell him that for a moment, everything was gone. Everything that had brought her happiness had just...vanished, without the slightest hint that he had ever come back for her. "On and off," she said, shrugging as if nothing had happened. "But one thing's for sure—I cannot wait to get this cast off."

Philip placed a hand on her cheek and looked at her.

Was it longing? Sadness? Did he pity her? The last thing she wanted was to be pitied. She'd had a good life. All in all, she had little to moan about and everything to be grateful for. She'd been blessed. Even Warren's lovechild had become like her very own. Abby had brought new meaning into her life and she was proud to call Abby her daughter. Her one regret would be that perhaps, just maybe, she should have tried harder with Madison.

"I love you," he said.

Louise studied him, tracing her finger along the lines on his face. She looked into his warm, inviting eyes. They were the kind that smiled at you from a distance. Laugh lines surrounded them, telling of a happy heart. His smile had always made her weak in the knees.

"What have I ever done to deserve you?" she mused. As a teenager, when Philip left for seminary school, Louise felt as if the world had ended. The betrayal hit her hard and fast. She'd focused her energies and anger towards God. And yet, God had brought him back to her. Forty years later. Was it too late?

Philip took her hand and gently kissed it.

"One day," she said, "all this will be a distant memory." Louise wondered what his life overseas was like. Had he been with other women before he'd come back to her? She wondered whose skin his hands might have caressed and whose lips had tasted his. What lucky woman had warmed his bed all those years ago? She dared not ask. It was years gone by. It was his past, and she had hers. But it ached her to know that they wouldn't have a future.

"Don't say that," he said.

She ran her fingers down his cheek and blinked back the tears that threatened her strength. "When the fog comes and envelopes all my memories, I want you to look the other way and keep going. Go far away and don't look back."

Philip, still holding her hand to his lips, closed his eyes.

"Promise me, Philip," she urged him. "Promise me you won't stay to see me disappear." She'd never seen Philip cry. She leaned in and kissed the tears that she knew he tried so hard to keep inside.

Chapter 24

Sarah Gardner

The weeks passed, and things went from bad to worse. Sarah had taken a leave of absence from her job at the church to stay home with Noah, who she'd pulled out of school. His outbursts of anger and self-focused behavior had become too much for his teachers to manage, and they'd insisted he see a specialist for behavior therapy and medication. But to Sarah, it wasn't that simple. The options overwhelmed Sarah and she found herself frozen, unable to make a decision.

When they'd first started, Sarah used to take Caleb along to the specialist appointments; but over time, she slowly began keeping information from him.

"When is Noah's next appointment?" Caleb asked Sarah as she prepared dinner.

Sarah didn't look up from the chopping board. "I'm waiting to hear back from the doctor's office," she said.

Caleb took an apple from the fruit basket and rubbed it against his shirt before taking a bite. "Still? What are they waiting for? There seems to be a lot of time in between appointments. Do you want me to find out what's going on?"

The crunch of the apple, as Caleb bit into it, annoyed Sarah. In fact, every bit of noise grated at her. Her patience was virtually non-existent, and she found excuses to stay away from having anything to do with people. Sarah brought the chopping board over the stove and slid the onions into the pan. The onions sizzled as it touched the hot surface, giving Sarah a moment to think of an answer. She reached for a spatula and pushed the onions around. "I don't know. I'll follow up with them in the morning." Sarah knew it was wrong to keep Caleb away, but she couldn't shake the feeling that he just wouldn't understand. Noah wasn't his real son, and she feared he'd make decisions that would suit him—rather than what was best for Noah.

"Any tantrums today?" he asked.

Sarah took three cloves of garlic and smashed them with the back of the knife. "They're not tantrums, Caleb. I asked you not to call them that."

"My bad,"—Caleb took another bite—"any outbursts today?"

It was moments exactly like those that made her believe he didn't feel the same; him not being Noah's biological parent. She was Noah's mother, and it was her responsibility to make sure she made the right decisions for him. "These things aren't to be taken lightly," she said as she furiously chopped the garlic before adding it to the onions. She sprinkled salt and pepper over the garlic and gave it another stir.

Things were changing rapidly between them. She'd even taken to sleeping early, or going to bed late to avoid having to share any intimacy with Caleb. She just couldn't do it.

Sarah wished for the thousandth time that Adam was alive. He would have known what to do. He would have taken the same precautionary steps she was taking. They were a good pair—Adam and Sarah. Together, they would have researched the pros and cons of the various treatments available; or what effects the different medications might have on their son. Sarah felt she was all alone in this battle.

To Caleb, it was all about getting it done. Sign the dotted line and get the treatment underway. "He's not the only child with ADHD, Sarah," he'd said once. Sarah couldn't quite recall, but that might have been the time that she'd started keeping things from him.

"Noah might be just any child to you, Caleb, but not to me," she'd countered. "He's my child! He's my son!"

Caleb flinched, and Sarah knew she'd hurt him with her words. But it all boiled down to one thing, and that was Noah. She was his mother. He looked to her for love, nourishment, and safety. He looked to her for everything, and it was her responsibility to make the best decision for him.

"Mommy, I'm hungry," Noah said as he walked into the kitchen. "Caleb!" he beamed when he'd spotted him and ran towards Caleb to pick him up.

Caleb picked Noah up with ease and tousled his hair. "How's my little man?" he asked. "Did you do anything cool today?"

Noah shrugged. "I went to the doctor lady, and we played some games."

Sarah froze as soon as she heard what Noah said.

"Did you? You went to the doctor today?" Caleb asked.

"Yeah," Noah replied. "And she gave me a stamp because I did very well—see?" Noah held his hand up for Caleb to see.

Sarah didn't turn around. She couldn't. She'd been caught in lie and she knew it was going to lead to another argument.

"Why don't you go wash up before we have dinner?" Caleb put Noah down.

"But I'm hungry," Noah whined.

"It won't be long," Caleb said. "Go on and tell Liam and Zoe to do the same. Wash your hands well. Can you do that for me?"

Noah nodded and ran out of the kitchen.

"Do you wanna tell me about that?" Caleb asked. His voice was low and tense.

Sarah threw in some sliced chicken into the pan and stirred it once more before setting the spatula down. She could feel Caleb's eyes on her.

"Sarah, look at me," Caleb said.

She turned to find him glaring at her.

"I thought we were on the same page," he said. "And now I find out you're hiding things from me."

"He's my son, Caleb!" Sarah argued.

Caleb's frustration was apparent on his face. "You wanna go at this alone, Sarah? Well, you got it," he'd said. "By all means, knock yourself out." Caleb turned on his heels and headed straight out the door, slamming it behind him.

Sarah jumped when the door slammed. She's done it. She'd pushed away the one person who was truly on her side.

Chapter 25

Kate Morgan

The first of December came around and as much as Kate wanted to welcome the Christmas season with happiness and cheer, she just couldn't find it within her. She sat down at the dining table in Sarah's kitchen and took the cup of tea that was handed to her. "We need to do something," she told Sarah.

Sarah sat down across from her. "About Louise?"

Kate nodded. She was desperate. If there was anything she could do to save her friend, she would do it. But as much as she wanted to, she was powerless. Feelings of inadequacy confronted her at every corner.

"There's really nothing we can do," Sarah said. "It is what it is."

"But there has to be!" Kate's tears rolled down her face. Normally, the tears would have come from Sarah. But this time, it was Kate who shed them.

"Kate...I know how much she means to you," Sarah said. "She means a lot to me too, but there's nothing we can do about it. This is—this is beyond us."

Kate felt the anger rising within her. "How can you say that?" she blurted. "How can you just sit there and accept it?"

"Kate—" Sarah paused and closed her eyes. "I don't know what you want me to say. I have my own problems too; in case you've forgotten. Noah's having a tough time. And Caleb and I..."

"We have a lifetime to figure things out for Noah! Louise might only have a few months left!" Kate caught herself and brought a hand to cover her mouth. It was clear from Sarah's face how much her words had hurt her. "Sarah...I'm sorry. I am so, so sorry."

Sarah smiled weakly, her lips barely moving. "I know."

"I don't know what came over me—the words, they just came out," Kate rambled. "I would never—oh gosh, I sound like my mother."

"Don't worry about it. I know you didn't mean it." Sarah placed a hand over Kate's. "And just so you know, you're nothing like your mother," Sarah smiled. "We will get through this. Somehow, some way, we will. But we can't argue...not like this. And it's not what Louise would want for us either."

Kate nodded. "You know I love Noah—and Liam and Zoe, right? As if they were my own."

"I know," Sarah said. "Now, tell me, how are you doing? How are things with your mom?"

Despite everything else that Sarah was going through, she still managed to pause and ask how Kate was coping. Shame washed over Kate. It was as if someone had dumped a bucket of cold water over her head. Kate opened her mouth to speak, but a sigh came out instead.

Sarah made a face. "That bad?"

"Worse than I ever could have imagined," Kate scoffed.

"Why do you let her?" Sarah asked. "I mean—please, tell me if I'm out of line here—but she does not respect you at all, Kate. I've seen the way she talks to you. It's just not right."

"I know. Louise pointed it out too, remember? You're both right." Kate placed her elbow on the table and rested her chin on her hand. "But even if you're right, there's nothing I can do about it."

Sarah shook her head. "You just have to tell her to her face."

"But she's my mother," Kate said.

"So what? That doesn't give her the right to treat you like that. Louise hit it right on the money, Kate. Helen walks all over you. She's demanding and when she doesn't get her way, she throws a tantrum. She is the most narcissistic person I have ever met in my life. And I've seen it with my own two eyes. She's about as mature as Noah."

Kate flinched. Her mother had, on more than one occasion, embarrassed Kate in front of her friends. "I don't how to explain it...it's just. It's what's expected of me. That's what Filipinos do," Kate said. "It's a cultural thing. I mean...for as long as my mother is on this earth, it's my responsibility to look after her."

"She's a grown woman, Kate. I'm sure she can look after herself," Sarah said. "Look, I may be coming across as being mean, but believe it or not, I'm coming from a good place. But really, it's just not right."

"As kids, we were always taught that parents sacrifice their lives for their children. And when they get too old to look after themselves, then it becomes the children's turn to look after the parents."

"To a certain degree, yes; but not like this."

Kate sighed. "Can we please talk about something else? I can't deal with any more talk about my mom right now. As it is, she occupies nearly every inch of my life. I don't want her to dominate my conversations too."

"You're right. I'm sorry," Sarah said. "Where's Louise today? Have you heard from her?"

Kate nodded. "She's at home. She said she wanted to get some knitting done."

"You know, that time when she told us off—well, kinda told us off. When she told me I needed to stop crying so much..." Sarah paused.

"I know what you're going to say."

Sarah studied Kate's face. "What?"

Kate hesitated. She didn't like talking behind Louise's back. "It was harsh...but she means well. Her words keep ringing in my head too."

"I'll admit, I got a bit upset. But then I realized that, yeah...I cry way too much." A smile formed across Sarah's lips. She placed a finger on the corner of her eye. "See? It's starting again," she said with a laugh.

"You cry enough for the three of us and our troubles," Kate joked.

Sarah told Kate about the problems she'd been having with Caleb. "I just feel that he doesn't have Noah's best interests at heart," she said.

"But this is Caleb we're talking about, and I know for a fact that he loves your children more than anything in the world," Kate said.

"I just feel so lost; you know?" Sarah said. "I keep wondering what Adam would have done if he was still here with us today."

"You can't keep punishing yourself like that," Kate said. "There's no way you will ever know what Adam would have done. The thing to ask yourself now is what do you want to do?"

"I'm just so confused," Sarah muttered. "Here's me telling you what to do, and you're there telling me what to do." Sarah laughed. "What a bunch of losers, we are."

"You have us. And you have Caleb," Kate reminded her. "Now's not the time to be pushing him away."

"I think that's a bit too late...I've well and truly pushed him away, haven't I?" Sarah pushed her tears back.

"Don't you go crying on me right now," Kate warned jokingly. "You'll both have us crying in a minute!"

"Okay, even if I know you're right—I mean, I keep trying to tell myself the same about Caleb. But I just can't seem to let him in...I don't know," Sarah sighed. "Why does everything have to be so hard? Weren't the last few years hard enough?"

"I know, right?" Kate laughed softly. "I tell you—it's all because I broke that stupid mirror!"

"Yeah, it's all your fault," Sarah joked. "Darned mirror!"

"You might want to steer clear of me for the next seven years. I'm a walking pot of bad luck."

"At least we're in it together, right?" Sarah teased.

"There's no one else I'd rather be in the dumps with—that's for sure," Kate agreed. Despite everything that was going on, her heart was filled with gratitude for the bond of their friendship.

Kate's phone rang. She stood up and pulled it out of her back pocket. It was Abby. "Hey you!"

"It's me, Abby," she said.

"I know—what's up? Everything okay?" Kate asked. "It's Abby," she whispered to Sarah.

"No," Abby said. "Well, it's Louise. She's turned up at the bookstore."

Chapter 26

Abby Delaney

Abby didn't know what to do. Louise had turned up at the bookstore in her pajamas. It was only when Abby had pointed it out that Louise realized what she'd done.

Abby knew that things were going to change, but she didn't think it would change so quickly. It hurt to see Louise so disoriented and confused.

"Louise?" Abby knocked on the back-office door. "Is everything okay? Can I get you anything?"

"Just leave me alone first, Abby, please." Louise had locked herself in the office and refused to come out.

"I just—I'm just worried about you."

"There's nothing to worry about, darling," Louise said.

Abby put her ear to the door. It sounded as if Louise was rummaging through papers. "Can you please open the door? Just for safety's sake. I won't come in, I promise." Abby turned at the jingling of the bells above the main door. Kate ran in, followed by Sarah and Noah.

Abby stood behind the counter and crossed her arms over chest as she stifled a laugh. "What are you two up to?" Kate and

Sarah were both dressed in their pajamas. Kate even had a sleep mask over her head like a hair band.

Kate raised her arms to the sides. "It's pajama day!"

"Pajama day for you too, Noah?" Abby asked Noah who was dressed in a Spiderman onesie and a mask.

"I'm not Noah," he said. "I'm Spiderman!"

"Ooh," Abby whispered and tapped her forehead. "Silly me!"

"Silly, Abby," Noah laughed.

"Where is she?" Kate asked more seriously.

Abby pointed to the back office. "She won't let me in."

"Let us try," Sarah said.

"Are you seriously wearing fluffy slippers?" Abby chuckled, amusement all over her face.

Sarah stuck her tongue out playfully. "They're very warm and comfy."

"So long as it doesn't rain," Abby teased.

"How did she get here?" Kate asked Abby.

Abby spoke softly. She didn't want Louise to hear that they were talking about her. "She came in a taxi."

"Louise?" Kate knocked on the door. "It's Kate."

"Kate?" Louise's voice echoed from inside the office.

"And Sarah!" Sarah inched next to Kate, putting her ear to the door.

"What are you both doing here?" Louise asked.

"It's pajama day, remember?" Kate said. "We were going to get us some *Tea for Three* and cozy up by the fire at Dockside."

Abby shook her head as soon as she realized what Kate and Sarah were up to. She hoped that if she ever found herself in such a situation, that she would have friends as good as them. If she was clever enough, it was something that she would do for Shelby. And, come to think of it, she was sure that Shelby would do the same for her.

The door clicked and slowly opened. Louise held it ajar and peeked through. "Pajama day?" Louise asked.

Kate raised her arms to her sides once more and beamed. "Yup—pajama day!"

Louise tentatively stepped out of the office and looked around the store. The broad smile on her face said everything.

Abby looked with combined amusement and tenderness at the three of them, all standing in their pajamas—Louise in her red-checkered flannel pjs, Sarah in her pink stripped ones, and Kate in a navy-blue number with fluffy white sheep. They all looked cozy and warm. If anyone else were to see them, it would look like Abby was the one who'd missed the memo.

"Ready to get some *Tea for Three*?" Kate asked, holding the crook of her arm out for Louise.

Louise grinned and linked her arm with Kate's. She nodded. "I'm ready."

Chapter 27

Kate Morgan

Kate, Louise, and Sarah walked arm in arm to Dockside Café with little Spiderman trailing along behind them. Well, not quite arm in arm. Louise was still had her cast on and needed the crutches to get around. They got a few weird stares—mostly surprise and wonder—but all in all, people smiled approvingly at the three women.

It seemed to Kate that all the stars had aligned because when they got to the café, all but one table was taken. And it just happened to be the sofas next to the fire. "Perfect," she said as they all sat down to warm up.

Sarah put their orders for tea and club sandwiches to share before joining them. She spotted an afghan draped over the sofa and placed it over Louise's leg. "Comfy?" she asked.

Louise nodded. "Yes, thank you."

"Noah," Sarah turned her attention to the masked superhero, "do you want your coloring book and crayons?"

Noah nodded and got straight to work.

"It was a good idea to bring him a bag of activities," Kate said to Sarah.

"I thought it might help. I've been experimenting, trying to see what engages him," Sarah said.

They sat in comfortable silence for a few minutes, giving Kate the chance to take it all in. She looked at Louise, who stared at the fire, mesmerized, her face serene and her cheeks beginning to flush with warmth. For a brief moment, everything was just like it used to be. The three of them chatting over endless cups of tea and sweet treats. It warmed Kate on the inside, and if her heart could glow through her chest, one would see it was a bright and cheerful red.

"Thank you," Louise said, breaking the silence.

"What for?" Sarah asked.

"For coming for me...dressed in your pajamas, looking like idiots," Louise smiled.

Sarah smiled. "It was Kate's idea."

Louise wiped the corner of her left eye. "I love you girls," she said with a quiver in her voice. "There is no one else in this world I'd rather be doing this with than you two."

"I kinda like the idea of being in our pjs," Kate said. "I'll bet everyone else is thinking they'd like to venture out in their own warm onesies too."

"We might start a new club—Pajamas and Tea," Sarah added.

"Tea and Jammies has a better ring to it," Kate said.

Louise cracked a smile. "I like it too."

"I might just stay in my pjs forever," Sarah sighed and threw her head back dramatically. "The way things are going, I might never leave the house again."

Louise frowned. "What have I missed?"

"She and C had a big fight," Kate said.

"C? Oh, you mean—" Louise glanced at Noah, who had his head down as he colored over the lines. She nodded. "Right, I'm with you. What's happened?"

Sarah laid her head on Louise's shoulder. "You were right," she said. "I was a big *B*, and I blew it."

"A bee?" Louise asked.

"No, no,"—Kate jumped in—"a *B*."

"Oh!" Louise's face lit up. "A nasty piece of work you've been then, I see?"

Sarah sniffed. "I'm doomed to spend the rest of my life alone. Maybe we should all just move in together and call it a day."

"Uh-uh," Louise said, "I've got lots of plans, darling. Lots and lots to do, before it's all over."

"What kind of plans?" Kate asked.

Louise twisted her lips. "I don't know...I guess you could call it a bucket list."

"I like it!" Sarah sat upright. "I like the idea of a bucket list—count me in!"

"What? No," Louise crossed her arms. "I don't want to be responsible for you going off the deep end and doing something crazy."

"But I need crazy!" Sarah persisted. "You said so yourself. You said I need to stop crying so much—and by the way, I have to say you really hurt me when you said that."

"I didn't hurt you, darling," Louise said. "The truth did. I merely pointed it out."

"Fine. But I need to fly,"—Sarah spread her arms out—"fly like a bird."

Louise laughed. "In case you didn't know, dodo birds don't fly."

Kate watched Sarah and Louise bicker. "You're both dodos."

"I still have my senses," Louise said and then pointed to Sarah, "this one here, however, is questionable."

Sarah feigned shock. "I'm doing it," she said. "I'm making a bucket list. Come on, Kate, pick a side." Sarah wriggled her eyebrows at Kate, who smiled and shook her head.

"I'm with Sarah on this one," Kate said.

"Fine," Louise said. "But if she decides to jump out of a plane to spread her wings, I'm out."

They all laughed. The idea of doing something together, something without disorders, diseases, and cultural boundaries, was uplifting. In that very moment, everything was perfect. Kate wished she could hit the pause button and remain in the moment for a while longer.

Chapter 28

Louise Delaney

The following Friday, Louise decided to go with Abby to the bookstore. The last time she'd visited she turned up in her pajamas; and while it was funny to look back on it, it was a frightful experience. She hated to think what it might have done to Abby.

"Are you sure this is a good idea?" Abby asked as she took the crutches from Louise and helped her into the car. Philip had taught her how to drive, and she'd aced her driver's exam—unsurprisingly to everyone else but herself.

"I'll be fine," Louise held her breath in as she lowered herself into the passenger's seat. "Besides, I thought it would be nice for us to spend some time together when I'm not in my pjs," Louise grinned.

"Ha-ha, very funny," Abby said, rolling her eyes. "I'm just worried that you might be pushing yourself too soon." Abby shut the door and walked to the other side of the car.

"We can even close the shop for lunch and grab a bite to eat," Louise continued when Abby got in next to her. "What do you think?"

"Hmm,"—Abby checked her rearview mirror before pulling out of the driveway—"I've got Children's Time then."

"Oh, yes, that's right. Well, it will be lovely seeing you in action with the kids," she said. Louise tried to hide her surprise. Children's Time was yet another thing she'd forgotten about. Abby had organized a new lunch time session for parents with young children, reading them a new storybook each week after which she would give out photocopied pictures to color in. The half hour Abby invested had boosted sales for the shop as parents lingered for longer and purchased books for either themselves or their kids, while Abby read them stories and kept them occupied. Abby had been running the show solo, and it turned out that she had a good head for business. "I am so proud of you, Abby."

Abby shrugged. "It's nothing."

"It's not nothing," Louise assured her. "When you said you didn't want to go back to college, I was worried about what you would be doing."

Abby gave her a sideways glance and smiled. "Did you think I'd be lounging about and become a couch potato?"

"Well, no...not really. Okay, yes." They both laughed.

"I'd rather stay here with you—besides, who's going to look after you if I'm away at college?"

"The girls," Louise said. "And Philip."

"Sure, okay," Abby said. "But still, I want to be here in case..." she hesitated.

"In case I lose my marbles before you return and forget all about you?" Louise teased.

"Don't say that!" Abby protested.

"Oh, come on...lighten up, my love. I'm just teasing."

"I don't like it." Abby clenched her jaws, keeping her eyes on the road.

Despite the way Abby had come into her life, Louise was grateful for the girl. They'd had a rocky start to their relationship, but in the end, Abby managed to sneak her way into Louise's heart. "There's something I need to talk to you about," Louise said as they turned into Lighthouse Road.

Abby glanced at her. "What about?"

"We'll talk when we've got a moment today. How's that?"

Abby put her turn-signal on before pulling into a vacant parking space. "Should I be worried?"

"No, don't be silly. Why would you say that?"

"No reason," Abby said. She turned the engine off and stepped out of the car.

Louise opened her door and handed the crutches to Abby as she came around to her side. "I can't wait to see you with the children at story time."

"They're actually kinda cute."

"I never imagined you working with kids," Louise said. "But then again, you've always been so good with Sarah's kids, and now Kate's too. I think you'd make a great mother." It was heartbreaking to know that there was so much she would miss out on. Her own daughter Madison was on the other side of the world in New Zealand. It had been years since Louise had seen her, and she hadn't even met her new granddaughter yet. It pained her to know that her time with Abby was going to be cut short too.

"Do you ever think of—" Abby hesitated.

"Think of what?"

"Do you ever think of Madison?" Abby helped Louise out of the car.

"Every day," Louise said without pause. She'd started her list and one of the things she'd written down was to stop holding back—her thoughts, emotions, and wants. Life, as she'd learned, is too short to keep things bottled up.

Abby made a face. "Well, I'm still not having any kids!"

"Never say never," Louise warned. But she knew why Abby felt that way. The girl had a rough start in life. Her mother was a drug-user and an alcoholic. And there was her father—Louise's late husband, Warren—who was absent and, for the most part, living a double life.

"Eew."

In many ways, mature as she was, Abby was also still a child.

LOUISE GASPED AS SHE stepped into the bookstore. The Christmas decorations were all up and everything looked festive and bright. A scent of warm gingerbread and cinnamon wafted through the air. "What's that smell?"

"Cinnamon," Abby said, holding the door open. "Do you like it?"

Louise smiled and nodded. "It smells like Christmas."

"I bought a diffuser that sprays a mist when the door is opened. It's sensor-activated." Abby pointed to a small contraption attached to the wall. "It's called Christmas Eve."

"Oh, Abby, this is all just so amazing—it's gorgeous!" Louise used to be the one to put the decorations up, and she was glad to see that Abby had taken it upon herself to carry on with the tradition.

"Mrs. Jury next door, she told me that you usually put it up on the first week of December, so I thought I would do it too."

Tears came to her eyes. Louise reached for Abby and pulled her in for an embrace. "Come here, you," she said, clutching Abby close. "I'm so proud of you, honey; I really am."

"Okay, don't get all teary on me now, Mom," Abby said absently and quickly brought a hand to her mouth. "I mean—sorry."

Louise looked into Abby's beautiful eyes and smiled. "That's the first time you've ever called me mom."

Abby's cheeks flushed. "I'm sorry, I didn't mean to—"

"I like it," Louise said as she smiled and nodded slowly. "I really do." At that moment, Louise felt her heart bursting with both love and sadness. She blinked back the tears that welled up in her eyes. But then she remembered her list and let the tears flow freely. No more bottling things up. She wanted to really acknowledge how she was feeling in that moment. Her heart was happy and her tears were ones of joy and love. "I love you, darling girl," she said.

"Uh—you can stop crying now," Abby said, her eyes looking everywhere else but at Louise.

"It's called the waterfall effect." Louise wiped her tears.

"It's called 'Mom's gone sappy.'"

"Mom...I like that," Louise smiled, pulling Abby back in for a hug.

"I like it too," Abby said, her voice muffled as she returned her stepmother's embrace.

Chapter 29

Abby Delaney

She didn't mean to call Louise mom. But in a way, Abby was glad that she had. It was something that she'd always wanted to do, but she didn't know how Louise would react to it since Abby wasn't her biological daughter. She saw the way Sarah felt about Caleb not being Noah's real dad, and she felt intimated at the thought of Louise pushing her away too. "There's something I need to tell you," Abby said after she'd properly opened the bookstore and turned the door sign to OPEN.

Louise looked up from armchair where she sat next to the Christmas tree. She'd brought a bag of knitting along to keep her preoccupied during the day and had already begun a row. "Mm-hmm?"

Abby walked behind the counter and pulled out three books from the shelves underneath. "My mother got in touch with me."

A few moments of silence passed before Louise said anything. "Rachel?"

Abby nodded and pretended to scan the books she'd pulled out. "These are the books I'm going to read to the children later on," she said. "Do you wanna see them?"

Louise ignored her question. "What did Rachel say?"

Abby knew it wouldn't be an easy conversation, which is probably why she'd waited this long to tell Louise about it. Rachel—her mother—was the one her dad had a one-night stand with. Abby shrugged. "She just wanted to know how I was doing."

"I see," Louise said softly. "Is she...in town?"

"She was; but she went back to Portland that same day."

"Did you see her?" Louise kept her hands moving as she continued to knit.

Abby nodded. "She'd sent me a text and asked if we could meet at Dockside Café." Abby hesitated, but then continued. "At first, I wasn't sure I wanted to go. So I talked to Shelby about it and we both thought that I might regret it later on if I didn't." Abby shrugged. "So I went. I asked Shelby to come with me—I guess I was too scared to go see her on my own."

"Oh, Abby, I wish I'd known. I would have been there for you." Louise set the knitting on her lap. "I mean, if you'd wanted me to; I'd have been there for you."

"I know," she said. "But I didn't want to burden you with it. Besides, Shelby was with me."

"What did your mom say?"

Abby avoided Louise's eyes. "She's no longer my mom," she mumbled. "You are."

"I'm sure you don't mean that."

Abby wiped a stray tear. "Yes, I do. She might be my mother, but you're my real mom."

Louise sighed and tucked her knitting back into her bag. "Do you want to tell me what you talked about?"

She didn't want to talk about it—but then also; she did. "She'd just come out of rehab," Abby said. "She said she quit drinking and using drugs."

"Well, that's wonderful news, isn't it?"

"A little too late, if you ask me." All her life, the only thing that Abby ever wanted was for her mom to pay her some attention; to show Abby that she loved her. Rachel didn't even bat an eyelid when Abby had left to live with Louise—a decision which hadn't been easy for Abby to make. In the last three years that Abby had been gone, Rachel had never even tried to contact her. Abby thought she'd gotten over it. But her sudden reappearance had ruffled Abby's new life, and she hated her for it.

"You know, Abby, as you get older, you'll find that we do a lot of stupid things. You may even do some of them yourself," Louise said. "I know it sounds like a cliché, but life doesn't come with a manual, honey. We're all just trying our best to get by."

"Well, she should have tried better—with me. I was her daughter. She shouldn't have let me go. I needed a mother."

"Earlier on, you asked me if I ever thought about Madison, and I told you that I did. I think about her every day," Louise said. "Like your mother, I shouldn't have let Madison go. Not without telling her that I love her and how proud I am of her. I guess what I'm saying is, I understand how you're feeling, and I think I can understand a little of how Rachel might be feeling as well. I know it hurts. And it will hurt for a long time. But maybe—just maybe—one day, you might find it in your heart to forgive her."

Abby looked up at Louise. "Is that what you want?" she asked softly, afraid of the answer. "Do you want me to forgive her and go back to her?"

Louise smiled.

Her smiles always comforted Abby. She'd never known how many things a smile could convey until she'd met Louise, Kate, and Sarah. The three women had been an integral part of her life, and they taught her what it meant to love and be loved. To Abby, Louise's smile was a like a hug that healed and soothed. It welcomed and warmed her, and made her feel like she was safe; made her feel like she was home.

"No, that's not what I'm saying. But if that's what you want to do; if you want to go back home, then I can't stop you. You're nearly an adult, after all. What I am saying is that I don't want you to live your life carrying such a heavy grudge. Those things are like cancer. They will spread through you quickly and before you know it, you are consumed with a hate so strong that you begin to dislike everything...even yourself. That's not what I want for you, my sweet girl."

Abby bit her lip. "This is my home now. And besides, it's not like she's asking for forgiveness or anything. So it doesn't really matter."

"Asking for forgiveness is difficult for lots of people," Louise said. "But you...you don't need her to ask you for forgiveness in order for you to forgive."

Abby looked up at the sound of the jingling of the bell. It was Shelby.

"Hello you two," Shelby beamed when she saw Louise and made a beeline straight for her, giving her a small hug.

"You're late," Abby joked. Since they'd become friends in high school, Shelby had become almost part of their little family. Louise had welcomed her, just as she welcomed everyone else—without judgement and without asking for anything in return. Abby knew that Shelby idolized Louise. She looked to her as a mother, seeing as neither of her parents wanted to know her.

"I can't be late if I'm not on the payroll," Shelby teased in return. She took her backpack off and brushed her purple hair with her fingers. "I think I need a haircut." She turned to Louise. "What do you think?"

"I like your hair like that," Louise said as she pulled her knitting out of the bag once more.

Shelby posed for Louise, showing her left profile, and then her right. "You don't think it's getting too long?"

"Not at all. And you get to do more things with it when it's longer," Louise said. "Now, tell me, Shelby. Where did you sleep last night?" It was always one of the first questions that Louise asked each time she saw Shelby. Louise had been trying to get her to move in with them ever since Shelby had saved enough for a small car and moved out of her parent's house.

"I parked up at the Village Park," she said. "It's nice and quiet after everyone has gone home."

"Shelby Rose, that is not good for a young woman to be sleeping out in the park! It's not safe," Louise protested. It was always the same scene. Louise scolded Shelby and then offered her the spare room at home. Shelby ignored the well-meaning words and politely declined.

"I'm fine, Mrs. D," Shelby said. "Really, I am."

"I don't care if you're fine or the queen of England—you're coming home with us tonight. And I don't want to hear another word about it." Louise ended the conversation and got back into her knitting.

Shelby glanced at Abby, who shrugged.

Louise looked back up at the both of them. "If you don't get Shelby to come home with us tonight, then I'm throwing you out to live with her on the streets, so at least you can look after each other," Louise threatened Abby.

"You heard her," Abby said to Shelby.

Shelby made a face. "But—"

"One day, I'll be too sick to even remember this conversation, and then where will you live?" Louise blurted. "It's best to move in now so that it stays in my head."

"That's not fair—you can't use the A-card," Shelby argued, laughing.

"I can and I did," Louise said sharply. "And it's called Alzheimer's, Shelby. You need to learn to say it. Now if you don't mind, I'd like to get back to my knitting please. I've had enough chatter for one morning."

Abby felt a pinch in her heart. Alzheimer's—what a stupid thing. Why do bad things happen to good people? It was unfair. Life was unfair. She could go to college another time. But for the time that Louise had remaining, Abby wanted to spend that with her. With *her mom*.

Chapter 30

Sarah Gardner

"I think we need to take a break," Sarah told Caleb after the kids were all in bed. She'd been thinking about it for a while now. It was as if all the parts of her had been taken and allocated, that she had none to spare for him.

Caleb continued washing the dishes.

"Did you hear me?" she asked softly.

Sarah watched as he turned the tap off, dried his hands on the kitchen towel, and turned to face her. "Yeah, I heard you," he said.

Her heart banged against her chest. "I'm sorry," she said, a feeble attempt at easing the blow.

"Are you?" Caleb made no attempt to hide what he was feeling. It looked to Sarah as if he'd been kicked in the stomach. She'd put too much on him; she'd been unfair to him. Sarah wanted him to yell at her. To tell her that she was making a mistake. She wanted to know how he was feeling. Instead, he calmly said, "Taking a break is not going to make things any easier, Sarah."

He was right. Of course he was right. "I just feel that I need some space—to think," she added hurriedly. "There's so much going on right now and I can't give you what you need."

Caleb shook his head and scoffed. "I don't need anything, Sarah. You're all I want. Why can't you understand that?"

Sarah averted his gaze. She hated that he was so calm. Why was he so calm? Where was his passion? If he loved the kids so much, then why wasn't he fighting for them? She wanted him to hurt her back, just as she was hurting him.

"Couples don't need to take a break to think, Sarah. Love is a choice. We made a commitment to each other. And that means for better of worse, through thick or thin, or whatever the heck you wanna call it. At least, that's what I did." Caleb hung the kitchen towel back on the hook by the sink. "I thought we were on the same page."

"We were—we are," she said.

"No, it doesn't look like we are. Just...for once in your life, make up your mind. Make a decision and stand by it!" His voice filled the kitchen. "I know you wish that life had this big manual of how to do things. That you could just look up how to get to the next level when you have no idea what to do. But that's not way it is. Yeah, life sucks sometimes. But life can be good too if you let it." Caleb leaned on the kitchen counter, his hands gripping the edges. "You can't keep doing this. You can't keep pushing me away every time we hit a bump in the road."

"Caleb,"—she took a step forward—"it's just that..." It's just what? Even she didn't know what she was thinking.

"It's just what?" His voice was composed. He didn't shout. There was no anger. Or tears. Nothing. "It's just that I'm not Adam. Is that what you wanted to say?"

Sarah felt her heart drop to her stomach. Caleb had hit the nail on the head. He wasn't Adam. And he was never going to be Adam. "Caleb, please..."

"Everything I do, Sarah—you compare me to him." Caleb's voice cracked. It was a brief moment, a sign of the hurt she was causing him. He sniffed sharply. "I can't compete with some-one you've put on a pedestal, Sarah. You still wear your wedding ring, and I haven't said a word about it, because I respect what you two had. But Sarah, when are you going to show me that same respect? When am I going to be enough for you?"

Her tears betrayed her like they always did. It was one of her many weaknesses. She was never good at hiding her feelings.

"When is it gonna get through your head that I love those kids just as much as you do? And when are you going to see that I love you?" Caleb fixed his eyes on her.

Tell him you made a mistake, she thought to herself. Tell him you didn't mean it.

"You're right," he said finally. Caleb ran his fingers through his hair. "We need a break."

Sarah swallowed her tears. "Caleb..."

"No, Sarah. You want a break? Well, you've got it. I'm not going to beg you. I'm not going to let you manipulate me in this twisted game of yours." Caleb shook his head. "I'm never gonna measure up to Adam." Caleb held her gaze. "You know—what we have, Sarah—it's not just a rebound thing for me. I know you're hurting. I know you didn't want Adam to die. No one did! But it happened. Did you forget that I was hurting too? Heck, I lost someone too!" He shook his head. "I'll pack my things and get out of your way tonight."

Panic filled Sarah's chest. This was what she wanted, wasn't it? Then why was she floundering? Why did it suddenly feel so wrong?

"Tonight? Caleb, you don't have to go tonight." She was pleading. Don't beg, Sarah, she thought. What happened to the bucket list? What happened to spreading her wings and being brave?

"I've made my choice. It's time to make yours."

"No, Caleb—"

"It's better that way," he said. "It's what you wanted, isn't it? Then you can have all the time you need to think. And when you're done; when you're well and truly done thinking, then let me know. I can't keep doing this with you." With that, Caleb walked out of the kitchen.

Sarah tried to slow her breathing. She closed her eyes, pins and needles ran along her lips. Breathe. She couldn't breathe. What had she done? "Caleb!" she raced out of the kitchen and up the stairs to the bedroom they shared; the bedroom that was once hers and Adam's. On the bed was Caleb's duffle bag—the same one he carried when he'd first moved in to help her with the children; that time when she was broken, and he'd helped her to pick up the pieces, one by one. But she was still broken. She was a mere fraction of who she'd been. Sarah had no idea who she was without Adam. And now, without Caleb... "Caleb, don't go." She clutched at his wrist as he reached into the drawer for more clothes. "Please don't go. I've made a mistake. Please don't go."

Caleb didn't snatch his hand away, instead, he gently took her hand off. "It'll be better this way. You need to think about what we are to each other, Sarah. About who I am to you. I can't have you breaking up with me every single time something goes wrong. We're not kids. That's not how this works."

"I'm sorry, Caleb—please." Tears ran down her face, her nose already stuffy. "It's me. It's all me, it's all my fault."

Caleb took her by the shoulders, willing her to look at him. "It'll be okay, you hear me? Just take the time you need. And when you're ready—when you're really certain—I'll be waiting."

Sarah closed her eyes as Caleb kissed her on the forehead. It was a soft kiss. Not one that spoke of passion or lust. It was a kiss much like one that a parent gave to their child. A kiss of love, one that spoke volumes—that promised to be there, no matter what.

"I'll be waiting." Those were Caleb's last words before he slipped out of her life.

Chapter 31

Kate Morgan

Christmas dinner was at Louise's house that year. She wanted to host what she called her holiday-shebang. "I want to create as many memories that I can hang on to," Louise had said. Kate didn't have the heart to tell her that even those would be taken from her.

She handed Adam to Mark, who had just arrived. "How are your parents?" she asked.

"Good," he said. "They were sorry to know we couldn't join them for dinner tonight, but I said we would try to visit them tomorrow, if that's okay with you."

Mark's visits to the house had become few and far between. It didn't help that Helen was outwardly rude to him. Kate was surprised that he hadn't yet left her after everything he'd had to put up with.

"Why are we doing it at her place?" Helen joined them in the living room. "I still think it's wrong that we didn't have Christmas Eve dinner. Do you remember, Kate? *Noche Buena* is an important part of our Christmas celebrations."

Noche Buena is a feast shared on the night before Christmas—but it isn't just a regular dinner. Every year on Christmas

Eve, Filipino families everywhere attend a midnight mass and then partake in a *Noche Buena* feast. It's a celebration of great cultural and religious significance.

Kate had to admit, she did miss the Filipino Christmas traditions. It was something she used to look forward to each year. The first day of September was officially the start of the *ber* months or better yet, the Christmas Season. Septem*ber*, Octo*ber*, Novem*ber*, Decem*ber*. It was when the malls began playing Christmas songs over the speakers, festive decorations and beautiful lanterns popped up all over the country. And on Christmas Eve, families gathered to celebrate the gift that is Christ himself.

"I told you—she wants to create memories," Kate finally said.

"Memories? That'll be a bit problematic, won't it?" It didn't matter how simple Helen's words were; they were quick and sharp, rarely well-meaning.

Kate glanced at Mark, who busied himself with Adam, and then back at Helen. "Why do you do that?" Kate asked. She was finally beginning to see the toxicity that was her mother. Her chest tightened, every breath rising with anger.

"Do what?" Helen opened her compact mirror and raised her eyebrows. "Can you do my eyebrows before we go?"

"Why do you have to be so mean?"

Helen clipped her mirror shut. "I'm just calling a spade a spade," Helen shrugged. "What's mean about that? It's the truth and sometimes, the truth hurts."

She'd heard that same line from Louise before. "I didn't hurt you, darling," Louise had said to Sarah. "The truth did. I merely pointed it out." But somehow, it didn't ring quite so viciously like Helen's words did. "I know that—but you don't have to say it like that. I mean, why even say anything?" Most parents taught their children that if you don't have anything nice to say, then it is better to say nothing at all. Kate, however, was taught to speak up; which, in the right context, would be good. But Kate had never learned to speak up. Words evaded her, afraid to cause anyone the same hurt that her mother caused her. Kate's inability to quickly articulate herself was yet another cause for disappointment for Helen, who had always wanted Kate to be a debate champion just like she was. Everything that Helen was...was everything that Kate wasn't. Helen was bold and gregarious, whereas Kate was timid and shy. Helen was petite and well-shaped; and Kate was tall and overweight.

"*May plano ang Diyos para sa lahat*, Katherine. It's not for us to question his plans."

God has plans for everyone. They were wise words that, in the past, would have comforted her; but not this time. Kate's anger rose at the mention of God's plans. What kind of God would lay such a sentence of someone as good as Louise? Louise was the most kind, caring, and compassionate woman Kate had ever known. What kind of God would do that? "You mean the God who had maliciously infected her with such a terrible disease that she forgets everyone who ever loved her? Forget how to eat? To drink? The God who so callously has left her to die a slow and undignified death?"

Helen's face contorted beyond recognition. Her dark eyes narrowed at Kate and her lips formed to deliver a lashing.

"Katherine Ann! You are not to speak that way of the Lord," she shouted.

Adam wailed in fright and Mark hoisted him up from the playpen.

"Is that what you've become?" Helen spat. "How dare you question the Lord—you should be ashamed of yourself!"

Kate had had enough. "Why did God choose someone like Louise? Why couldn't he have chosen you instead?" The words came out, lashing, scathing.

Helen's eyes widened. "How dare you!"

"Uh—look guys, it's Christmas," Mark said as he comforted Adam. "Maybe you save this for another time."

"Exactly! It's Christmas," Helen snapped, "and you have the gall to speak ill of the Lord? *Patawarin ka sana ng Diyos*, Katherine."

May God forgive her. Kate took a deep breath and took Adam from Mark. "It's okay, Adam, Mommy's here."

"Kate, just leave it," Mark said softly. Since Helen arrived, Mark had seen countless arguments between mother and daughter. It embarrassed her to have anyone witness it. It was like she was a child being reprimanded in front of her school friends.

She decided to bite her tongue, if only for Adam's sake. "I don't want to talk about it anymore," Kate said to Helen. "It's upsetting Adam."

But Helen continued. "You think just because you're now in America—that you're better than everyone else? *Ang yabang mo!* You're arrogant and incorrigible." She went right up to Kate's face—so close that Kate could smell the anger in her breath; the spit burning her skin. "You disgust me! Your father would be turning in his grave if he knew what you've become!"

Each word stung Kate; each one, a fresh paper cut. Slash. Sting. Slice. "What exactly have I become, Mother?" It was no longer about God, no. The argument, like all those before, had morphed into something Kate did not understand. Kate was in a fight ring with her mother, and Helen was determined to win.

"You've sold your soul and you don't even know it!" Helen hissed.

"Okay, that's enough," Mark said. "This isn't the time nor place to—"

"And you!" Helen turned her attention and rage to Mark. "Have you no shame? How dare you wreck a family!"

"Whoa!" Mark raised his hands as if in surrender.

"Ma!" Kate warned.

"Katherine—*wala ka bang nitirang kahihiyan?* Have you no shame?" Helen spat. "You're a married woman! And a mother! How could you allow this piece of white trash to ruin your marriage?"

"I'm divorced, Ma! And Mark did not—"

"Divorce is illegal! In the eyes of the Lord, there is no such thing as divorce. Have I taught you nothing? Your father and I were married for twenty-seven years, Katherine. *Twenty-seven years,*" Helen stressed. "You gave it what? One year?"

"Helen," Mark stepped in between the two women, "that's enough."

"Helen? Helen? How dare you call me that!" She was livid. "Have you no respect for your elders? *Ano'ng tinuro sa 'yo ng mga magulang mo?*"

"What?" Mark made a face.

"What have your parents taught you?" Helen repeated.

"Whoa—I think you should stop right there. Don't go bringing my parents into this—whatever this is." Kate could see that Mark was trying to keep his cool.

But there was no stopping Helen; not when she was on a roll. "Do your parents condone your relationship with a married woman?"

Mark looked at Kate. "I'm sorry, Kate," he said. "This is not going to work. Not if you allow her to stick her nose in everything."

Kate put a hand on Mark's arm. "Mark, I'm sorry—"

"My nose?" Helen continued. "She is my daughter!"

"And she is an adult, and she is my girlfriend," Mark argued.

"Not if I have any say in the matter." Helen glared at him.

"You don't." Mark took one last look at Kate. He raised both his hands up in front of him. "You gotta sort her out, Kate."

"No one is going to sort me out, young man! Bastos!" Helen was relentless. "You know what I just said? I said, you're rude! Bastos! It's you who needs sorting out."

"Ma," Kate pleaded. She was losing the battle—just as she always did. The boxing bell was a few seconds from ringing. "That's enough."

"I'm sorry, Kate," Mark said finally. "I didn't sign up for this kind of crazy. You choose—it's me or her."

"Get out!" Helen screeched, her eyes as wide as saucers, saliva gathered at the sides of her mouth like a rabid animal.

Mark looked at Kate.

"Katherine Ann, I swear on your father's grave, I will disown you!"

Kate seized; tears filled her eyes. Her ears rang, and the room began to spin. She let out a sob, and with that lone sob, Mark walked away. Away from her. Away from her crazy mother. Away from her life.

Merry Christmas.

Kate turned to Helen. Three words. She had three simple words for her. "I hate you."

Helen scoffed. "*Brava*, Katherine!" She laughed maniacally and clapped her hands. "*Brava!*" she spat.

Chapter 32

Louise Delaney

Louise took a step back to admire the dining table. With the help of Abby, Shelby, and Philip, they had adorned the walls with Christmas decorations, surplus to those on the tree. Together, they'd made a roast beef, twice-baked potatoes, and an apple and pear salad with pomegranate vinaigrette. The girls also prepared a giant cheese ball and scattered a variety of crackers around the platter. At the request of Louise, Philip had prepared a sticky date pudding drizzled with homemade caramel sauce.

Louise decided to use her best tableware—the ones she and Warren were gifted for their wedding. "There's no point in keeping them in the cupboards unused," she'd said as she pulled the set out. "One day soon," she told Abby, "these will be yours."

"Mom, can you stop saying things like that, please? I already told you I don't like it." Abby made it very clear that she didn't appreciate when Louise made any reference to her imminent mental decline.

"The sooner you come to terms with it, darling, the easier it will be to cope when it finally happens." Louise understood Abby's fears, and she wanted to, as best as she could, ease her wor-

ries. But she also wanted Abby to be realistic about what was
coming.

Earlier in the month, when Louise had spent the day with
Abby at the bookstore; unbeknownst to Abby, she had organized for a lawyer to meet with them. It wasn't difficult for
Louise to make the decision to put the bookstore in Abby's
name and leave it to her. Abby loved Chapter Five, and she was
so much better at running the business than Louise ever was.
She had arranged for a trust, giving Abby a monthly allowance
until she turned twenty-five years old, when she will be able to
gain full access to the deed and any additional inheritance. And
whatever monies remained from Warren's insurance, Louise had
split between Abby and Madison. It wasn't much, but she wanted no stone left unturned.

Abby had cried as she struggled to accept that one day soon,
Louise's mental faculties would deteriorate and that she may not
even recognize her own stepdaughter. But Louise held her close
and soothed her. "Don't worry," she'd said, "for God has a plan
for all of us, and I know in my heart that he will not desert you."

The other person who struggled with what was to come
was Kate. Poor, sweet Kate. They'd spent countless hours talking
about it—Kate pleading with her to get a second opinion, and
Louise explaining that she'd already had a second opinion, even
a third, and a fourth. Kate blamed God, and she was vocal about
her anger, pushing the boundaries; and Louise tried her best to
allay her fears. "Kate, I know it hurts. And it hurts because you
love me. But I've thought much about this, and I am now at
peace with it. I don't want to spend the time we have left arguing
about what we cannot change," she'd said to her best friend. "I

want to spend it with the people I love most. I want to be happy—to laugh and joke, to share meaningful conversations with you guys, keep ticking my bucket list until this disease finally takes over. We can't fight this, Kate. So please, from now on, let's talk about something else—anything but my Alzheimer's. Let's make the most of what little time we have left together." Kate said nothing. And from that day on, the A-word was never raised.

AFTER EVERYONE HAD complimented the festive table spread, they all sat down to dinner and Louise raised a glass. "Thank you for choosing to spend this special evening with us." She looked around the table, meeting each person's eyes, noting that Kate appeared troubled. "As you know, I wanted to host this Christmas dinner so that I could cherish this time with you. I'm happy to see that everyone I love is here,"—she made a mental note to ask Kate where Mark was—"and my heart is filled with gratitude. Here's to you, my favorite people in the world."

Cheers erupted, and Christmas wishes were exchanged across the table.

"Philip, darling," Louise put a hand over his, "would you lead us all in prayer, please?"

Philip nodded and bowed his head, as everyone reached for the hand of the person next to them. Silence hung over the table.

"This Christmas, we thank you, dear Lord, for the gift of your son Jesus," Philip began. "We thank you for the gift of one another, and the chance to celebrate tonight in your holy name." Philip closed his eyes. "From the book of Psalms chapter 119 verse 105, Your word is a lamp to my feet and a light to my path. The future is always unsure. Rarely do we get to see the view to the horizon. But God's words of faith, hope, and love are a lamp for our feet, lighting the next step on the path before us. For we do not know what the future holds," said Philip, "but we know the one who holds our future."

Louise didn't close her eyes. Instead, she looked at everyone seated around her—the friends who have become her family, the kids who had become her grandchildren. She saw Kate breath a heavy sigh.

"Lord God, we ask that you be present with us now, in this moment when we are together, and help us to walk with you, even when the way seems dark." Philip's voice drifted across the room.

Kate reached for a tissue in her pocket and dabbed at her tears.

Lord, please bless Philip for his kind and healing words, Louise thought.

"May hope be born anew in us," Philip continued. "May your peace rest with us. May love abound," he said, "and may joy be reawakened. Amen."

Spring

Your children are not your children.
They are sons and daughters of Life's longing for itself.
They come through you but not from you.
And though they are with you yet they belong not to you.
~Kahlil Gibran

Chapter 33

Kate Morgan

It had been two months since Kate had last seen Mark. It had hurt her that their relationship had ended so abruptly. It felt unfair to Kate that Mark had made her choose between him and her mom. As much as she'd wanted to, there was no way that she could choose him over her mother. The path to becoming a dutiful daughter was a difficult one for Kate, for in choosing her mother over Mark, hatred burned within her.

"Love is a commitment," Louise said. The three of them had decided to spend the afternoon at the Dockside Cafe—for old time's sake—to share some *Tea for Three*. "Have you ever heard of that saying—'If you love someone, set them free. If they come back, they're yours; if they don't, they never were'?"

Kate nodded. It was an old saying that has popped up time and time again.

"Looks like it was never meant to be, darling," Louise said.

"I agree with Louise," Sarah said. "And it goes both ways. Look at me and Caleb. I do love him, but I guess I wasn't in it as much as I thought I was. Otherwise, I'd ask for him to come back."

"So you've definitely broken up?" Kate asked Sarah. It was sad—there was no other way to put it—that all of their relationships have gone south, except for Louise and Philip's of course. She wished that she could have a relationship like theirs. It was obvious to anyone that Louise and Philip were very much in love and made for each other.

Sarah paused and took a sip of her tea. "I miss him a lot. I would be lying if I said I didn't."

Louise shifted in her seat. "Have you called him?"

Sarah shook her head. "He was right. I kept comparing him to Adam, and it wasn't fair on him or anyone else for that matter. I need to take a step back and really think about our relationship. We started too soon after Adam's death. I don't think I had enough time to really grieve or even process my own feelings."

"That's the smart thing to do," Louise said.

"What's happened to us?" Kate mused. "I just can't believe how much things have changed in just a year's time. At least you've got your happily ever-after," she said to Louise.

Louise smiled and raised her eyebrows. "But do I?"

"Oh gosh, Louise, I'm sorry. That was very insensitive of me." Kate wanted to kick herself. What a stupid thing to say. The weather was lovely, and the sky was the brightest of blues. If one looked at Louise, they would never know there was something more sinister going on inside. But this, the three of them together, was pure happiness—despite the conversations they were having, broken hearts and all. Once more, Kate wished that she could stop time and just hang on to the moment.

Louise took a deep breath in. "There's a time for everything. Simply put, mine is due soon. But I have you girls. I have Abby. And Philip. I'm the happiest I have ever been in years. So really, maybe I did get my happily ever-after," she said.

"Kate, can I ask you something?" Sarah asked.

"Sure," Kate said. "Anything."

"It's about your mom," Sarah said tentatively.

Kate could sense where the conversation was heading. She'd heard it many times before—from Sarah, Louise, Mark. Surprisingly, she'd also heard it from Evan. She knew they meant well, but they just didn't understand. Or maybe she just didn't know how to get out it.

"I know that culture has a lot to do with it, but don't you think that your mom has too much control over you?" Sarah asked.

Louise nodded. It was a small nod of agreement, but Kate saw it anyway.

Kate sighed. "I told you guys before, I can't just kick her out. She's my mother."

"It's not that you have to throw her out or anything like that," Sarah said. "But Kate, she has this really tight hold on you and I don't think you even know it."

"Honor your father and mother," Kate said. "That's what the bible tells us to do."

"Darling, if I may," Louise said. "This, coming from a mother; there are times when one must draw a line in the sand, if only to protect themselves and the ones they love."

Kate shifted in her seat and rubbed the back of her neck.

"I have watched you grow from a timid young woman into a strong and independent mother." Louise poured herself another cup of tea. "When your mother arrived, that strong woman all but disappeared. Poof! Just like that."

Louise was right. Kate knew it, and she felt it too. But what could she do? It wasn't as easy as everyone thought. She didn't know how to break away from her mother, without it appearing that she'd abandoned her. What would people say? What would her father say?

"You have been told, for years and years, as you say, to honor your father and your mother. And why not? They brought you into this world, raised you, fed and clothed you. But what do you do when that honor—that respect—is not reciprocated? You are a grown woman, Kate. And your mother needs to acknowledge that and be proud of who you have become." Louise gazed at Kate and smiled. "Just look at yourself, darling. If you were my daughter, I would be so proud of how independent you are. And how you are navigating this big world on your own."

"You yourself are now a mother," Sarah added. "This is the time for you to look at everything you've achieved and be happy. Take pride in it. And it hurts me because I can see that you aren't."

"Life is funny," Louise said. "You know, it is possible to love someone, and at the same time, to acknowledge that you cannot have them in your life. You need to look after yourself, darling, and your own mental health. You have a son now, and he needs you. I know it's terrifying. But sometimes, you just have to take a leap of faith."

Kate nodded thoughtfully. They were right. It was something she'd pondered on herself on multiple occasions. Caught between her traditional cultural values and the freedom of independence in the western world, Kate found herself torn. It was a constant battle for Kate; a battle of ethics, values, tradition, and culture.

If she was still in the Philippines, then she and her mother would have lived together. It was a given. Between them, they would have had household helpers to take all the chores away. In the Philippines, if you could afford it, there were live-in staff who looked after you—undertaking the gardening, the cooking and cleaning, and whatever else was needed. So it would be possible for Kate and her mother to live in the same house, share the same space, and still live fairly independent lives. But she wasn't in the Philippines anymore, and life in the United States was different.

The dilemma hung over Kate like a dark cloud, day in and day out, since her mother had arrived. Afraid as Kate was to admit it, she was caught in a web of firmly held familial traditions and religious values. It was an ongoing struggle for her as she tried to free herself from the cultural chains that kept her bound.

But what could she say? What could she do? How could she possibly turn her back on her mother? Kate pressed her lips together. It was so ingrained in her; it was a deep part of who she was. A knot formed in her chest and it felt as if her heart was going to explode.

Chapter 34

Louise Delaney

It was Saturday morning when there was a knock on the door. Louise, Philip, and Abby had just finished breakfast and were sitting outside on the back porch with their cups of tea. It was cute how, once upon a short time ago, Abby would only drink hot chocolate. And today, there she was, all grown up and enjoying a morning cup with the adults. "Are we expecting anyone?" Louise asked.

"I'll get it," Philip said as he made to get up.

"No," Louise put her hand up, "let me." Her cast had finally been removed, and walking in a moon boot made it much easier to get around. "I like practicing walking on this thing."

"I'll come with you," Abby said, getting up.

"It's just the door, love; you sit down and relax," Louise said.

Louise smiled as she hobbled towards the door. It was funny how Philip and Abby took turns fussing over her. She knew they meant well, but there were sometimes when she yearned for the days when getting up to answer the door didn't seem like such a big adventure. She ran her fingers through her hair and opened the door with a smile, expecting it to be one of the girls.

"Hi, Mom."

Louise opened her mouth to speak, but the words were stubborn and refused to come out. *Is it happening again?* she wondered. Am I in the other world? Louise brought a hand to her chest, her heart pounding wildly against it. She closed her eyes and took a deep breath before opening them once more.

She was still there.

"Madison?" Louise reached out to touch the woman who so resembled her estranged daughter. Tears pushed past her eyes. The dam that held them had finally broken. She touched her and felt the skin beneath her fingertips. And then she reached for her long, dark hair; winding the curls around her own fingers. There was no denying it. It was Madison.

Chapter 35

Abby Delaney

It wasn't hard to find Madison Delaney on Instagram. Abby had typed her name in and a few accounts popped up. As soon as she saw Madison's profile photo, she knew immediately that she was looking at her half-sister. Abby had browsed through her photos—photos of Madison with her daughter, with her husband, husband and daughter, flowers and plants, food, nature and a whole lot of sunsets. At a glance, it looked like Madison was living the perfect life. And why shouldn't she? Just because she was the daughter that Abby's father, Warren, had chosen; it didn't mean either one of them deserved less in life.

"What do you think?" Abby asked Shelby. Since moving in with Louise and Abby, they'd become closer than ever. It was like having a real sister.

"It's so weird that you guys look so much alike," Shelby said absently. "Can you see it? I mean, man, just look at that!"

"She does—I mean, like, I totally see myself in her." It was surreal for Abby to see herself in someone else. She wondered what Madison was like and if they had anything, other than a father, in common.

"That—is—awesome! You could be twins or something." Shelby scratched at the tip of her nose.

"Hmmm...I guess this means I'm an aunt." Abby enlarged the photo of Madison's daughter. "She's cute, huh? Do you think she'll answer me if I send a message?"

"Are you sure you wanna do it?" Shelby stretched out on the bed and leaned on her elbows. "Like, what if Louise gets mad?"

Abby thought about it. She'd been thinking about it for some time now, since their brief conversation at the bookstore. She also remembered that time when she'd found Louise crying in the garage two years ago. Abby knew that she had to do something—to reach out and let Madison know that their mom was sick. Their mom. "I think I have to do this. It might be the only chance we've got."

"Okay then, let's do it!" Shelby was Abby's best friend, and she did exactly what best friends were supposed to do. From the day they first met, they'd been each other's biggest cheerleaders.

Abby hit the message button and stared at the blinking cursor. "What should I say?"

"I don't know. Something like,"—Shelby paused to think—"Hiya...I'm your sister."

Abby made a face. "But that's like, so in-your-face."

"Well, then you think of something. You're the one who got into college, Miss Smarty-pants."

"Dear Madison," Abby typed and then quickly deleted it. "Hi Madison—" she stopped typing and looked at Shelby. "How's that?"

"Very Shakespearean," Shelby rolled her eyes. "Go on."

Abby pushed herself up and sat cross-legged on the bed, holding her mobile phone in both hands. She threw her head back and sighed. "Okay, let's do this."

Hi Madison

My name is Abby Delaney. You don't know me, but I'm Warren's daughter.

I know it's weird that I'm writing you, but I just wanted to let you know that Mom is sick. She's been sick for a while and I think that she might really want to see you.

I'm sorry if this comes as a shock to you, but I thought you might want to know.

Abby

"There," Abby said and passed her mobile phone to Shelby for her to read.

Shelby bit her lip as she read through the message. "Looks great," she said approvingly.

"Do you think that'll be alright?" Abby scratched the corner of her lip. "I mean, like, should I tell her more? What Mom has or something?"

Shelby shook her head. "If she wants to know more, then she can message you back."

"You're right. Great idea!" Abby said. "I'm sending it now."

"Go ahead, send it."

Abby hovered her finger over the send icon, closed her eyes, and tapped on it. She tossed the phone on the bed and covered her mouth. "I hope we've made the right decision."

ALL THROUGHOUT THE week, Abby kept going back to her Instagram inbox. She knew that Madison had seen her message. It said so on the bottom right-hand of the message, in italics—*Seen*.

It took a few days for Madison to get back to Abby. Five days. Well, five and a half days to be exact. Abby had been at work. It was a quiet time at the bookstore. She was doing an inventory of the greeting cards on the rack when she heard a notification ping on her phone. She glanced towards the counter and quickly retrieved her phone. It was a message from Madison.

Abby held the phone briefly to her chest and took a deep breath. "Please God, please God, please God," she murmured. She then blew out a long exhale and opened the message.

Hi Abby

Sorry for the delay in coming back to you. I'm sure you can appreciate that it took me some time to take it all in.

Wow! I have so many questions, I don't even know where to begin.

Firstly, thank you for letting me know about Mom. Do you know what specifically is wrong with her?

Cheers

Madison

Abby could see that Madison was still online. From her research, Abby knew the New Zealand was twenty-one hours ahead of Carlton Bay. She checked the time on her phone; it was 3:00pm. That meant it was 6:00pm, a day ahead, in New Zealand where Madison was.

She read the message again. She didn't have time to call Shelby and discuss what to do. Instead, she typed the message quickly.

She has Alzheimer's.

Abby hit send. She could see on the screen that Madison was typing a reply.

Typing...

Then it came. Madison had sent a message back.

How bad is it?

Abby told Madison everything she knew. There was no point in holding on to anything.

The doctor said that symptoms could worsen any time and that we can expect to see it happen sooner rather than later. It's early onset Alzheimer's. From what I understand, it moves at a quicker pace.

Abby watched the screen: *Typing...*

Does Mom know you messaged me?

Louise didn't know. Abby hadn't told her. For one thing, she wasn't sure if Madison would engage with her at all.

No.

When she didn't receive a message back, Abby sent another one.

She's been forgetting a lot of things lately. She's stopped going to work because she just can't manage whole days any longer. She also had a fall and was in a cast for a few weeks. But she mentioned, one time when we were talking, that she thought about you a lot...

And then finally, Madison sent the message Abby had hoped she would.

I'll come home as soon as I can.

Chapter 36

Sarah Gardner

Sarah walked along the dockside. She'd organized for a babysitter to look after Noah for a few hours while Sarah picked up some Christmas presents for the children. The dockside was bustling with activity and people were out and about. Sarah spotted a young family looking over the water. She stopped and smiled as the father carried a toddler on his shoulders, while the mother stood back taking a photo of them.

Sarah's thoughts traveled to Adam and the days when he would carry the children on his shoulders too. It was something he never got to do with Zoe. A hint of sadness colored Sarah's heart. They were happy, really happy.

She felt for the ring on her finger. It was their wedding ring—the same one she'd vowed never to remove. For better or worse, till death us do part. But death had parted them. Adam was gone. He would never get to play with his children again; or never hold Sarah in his arms again, making her feel like nothing could ever harm them.

The young father lifted the toddler off his shoulders and passed the little tyke to his mom. Happy squeals erupted from his little body, his legs kicking in anticipation, as his mother reached for him. Sarah felt a lump in her throat. She needed to find a way to get past all her feelings of guilt and fear. She had many memories of Adam—and they were hers to keep. It didn't mean that moving on meant that she loved him any less.

Caleb's voice echoed in her thoughts. I'll be waiting—those were his last words to her.

Sarah took a deep breath and then exhaled. In that exhale, she tried to let go of her fears, insecurities, and worries. Honesty. That's what she needed. She needed to be honest with herself. She was happy with Caleb too. Then it hit Sarah...it was okay to find happiness in someone other than Adam. Why couldn't she give herself permission to be happy?

Caleb was not the father of the children, but he loved them like they were his own. And more so, he loved her. Not once had she ever had any reason to doubt that. So why had she let it consume her?

Looking back, all the arguments they'd ever had were because of her own fears—her own mistrust of a man who wanted nothing more than to be with her; to love her.

It all started coming to her as if the sky was clearing.

Sarah hurried to her car and headed straight to the school.

AT THE SCHOOL, SHE checked her watch and knowing the students would be on their afternoon break; Sarah headed straight for the office.

Marnie, the office lady, looked up as she walked in. "Mrs. Delaney," she said with a smile, "how are you today?"

"Very well, thank you, Marnie." She meant it. At that moment, with clarity in her heart, she was very well, thank you, Marnie!

Marnie made a face. "Did someone call you about Liam?" With Noah no longer enrolled, Liam was the only Delaney at the school.

"No, actually—I'm here to see Caleb, if that's alright."

"Coach Myers..." Marnie voiced. "Do you have an appointment?"

"No, I just—"

"Hmm...let me see if he's in the staffroom; just a moment, please."

Sarah stepped away from the desk as Marnie picked up the phone. Ordinarily she'd have worried what Marnie might have been thinking. It was a small town, and no one was immune to a bit of gossip. But this time, she didn't care. She wasn't doing anything wrong. Death had parted both her and Adam. She had a bucket list, and she was determined to fill it up with happy experiences—daring ones, bold ones.

"Mrs. Delaney?" Marnie called to her. "Coach Myers is in the staff room, if you'd like to go ahead and see him."

"Thank you, Marnie," she said, clutching her purse.

"Do you know where it is?" Marnie asked.

Sarah nodded and walked through to the hallway. She stopped in front of the staff room and just as Sarah raised a hand to knock; the door opened. It was Caleb.

"Sarah—is everything okay?" he asked in a rush. Looking around. "Marnie told me you were here. Is it Noah?"

She placed a hand on his chest. "Everything's okay. Noah's fine," she said. "I—I actually came to see you."

Caleb took her by the hand and led her into the staff room. It was quiet, except for three, maybe four teachers, who nodded when they saw her.

He looked good. He'd grown a beard since she'd last seen him. It was neat and close to his face.

Caleb motioned to the old-fashioned jug on the counter next to the sink. "Cup of tea or coffee?"

Sarah shook her head and smiled.

They sat down on a small three-seater sofa. It was a faded orange and appeared to have been sat on by many different teachers over the years.

Sarah cleared her throat. She hadn't actually had time to rehearse what she should say to him. "I...uhm,"—she laughed nervously—"I'm sorry. I didn't quite think this through."

Caleb smiled, his gaze, tender. "Sarah..."

"I miss you, Caleb," she said, her voice trembling unexpectedly. "Day after day, I thought about you—and me. And the kids." Sarah wet her lips and bit the inside of her cheek. "We all miss you. I miss you. It's not the same without you," she said. "It feels like, once again, I'd lost someone that I truly love."

Caleb didn't say anything. His face was gentle as his eyes gazed into hers.

"I've been hard on myself." Sarah let out a quick breath—the one that was caught in her throat. "And in doing so, I projected that to you and the children. I was unreasonable, and I clung on to the past which I know will never see a future." Sarah twisted her wedding ring around her finger. "I was afraid of doing the wrong thing. I was afraid that if I committed Noah to a therapy program, that I would be agreeing that there was something wrong with him. I blamed myself for his condition, thinking that had it not been because of Adam's death, then he wouldn't be the way that he is. Or that because I have suffered from depression, that made him more inclined to develop some mental-related illness. I've been so ignorant and selfish and..."

"Sarah," Caleb sighed her name.

But she continued. "But you were right," Sarah said. "It's our responsibility to get him the help he needs."

Caleb nodded slowly, taking it all in.

Sarah felt her tears welling in her eyes.

Caleb cupped her cheek in his hand and placed his forehead against hers.

"I love you, Caleb. And I miss you so much." Tears spilled down her face.

Caleb pulled back and wiped her tears with his thumb. "I've missed you too—all of you," he said.

Sarah cracked a smile. "Please come home," she said.

At that moment, the door to the staff room burst open. A student rushed in, his face puffed and red. "Coach Myers! It's Cory—he's injured!"

"I have to go," Caleb said.

Sarah looked at him, her eyes pleading. "Caleb, wait—"

"I'm sorry," he said. As he got up, Caleb cast a quick glance at her and walked out the staff room.

She blew it. She'd lost her chance, and it was no one else's fault but hers.

Chapter 37

Kate Morgan

Kate went to work feeling less for wear. Every day, she'd go through the motions, almost robotically. She was exhausted and was having trouble keeping up with everything she needed to do. Having her mom stay with her had taken its toll on Kate. Helen never lifted a finger apart from doing the laundry. Helen had also found delight in scouring the thrift stores and was constantly bringing her purchases into the house. There were baby toys everywhere, baskets of different sizes, old books and magazines, throw pillows, mirrors, blankets; even pots and pans, which Helen never really cooked with, because cooking wasn't something she did.

"There's so much stuff in the house," Kate had said one day. That statement had turned into yet another argument that Kate just gave up and let her mother carry on.

And the music. Every time Kate arrived home from work, there was music blaring from a standalone speaker. Roy Orbison, Blink 182, Rod Stewart, Green Day, Metallica, Bach, Pachelbel, and Filipino church songs. Just like the things Helen brought back with her from her thrift shopping, the music she played had no real pattern to determine what she liked or didn't like.

It seemed to Kate like all the work she was doing was for nothing, because in addition to paying for all the household bills; she also had to pay Helen for looking after Adam.

"How else will I earn my own money?" Helen asked when Kate had raised her concerns. "You expect me to just depend on you? Ask you for money every time I need to buy something?"

Helen's presence drained her. Their relationship was tiresome and toxic. Kate had become afraid of her mother, in the same way that a teenager was. On one of the rare nights that Kate was going out on a date with Mark—when they were still in a relationship—she'd put two small hair clips on top of her head, pulling her hair away from her face. Helen had snorted and laughed at her. *"Mukha kang siopao."* Kate's heart had sunk that night. Her mother had just told her that she looked like a Chinese steamed bun. And even if she didn't want to; even if she knew that she would end up getting hurt, Kate had begun to look to her mother for her approval. It was like drawing a moth to a flame.

Kate's self-esteem had hit an all-time low. She'd even stopped eating after one evening, when she was cuddling Adam on the floor; Helen had told her to be careful because Kate was as heavy as an elephant and she was worried that Adam would suffocate beneath her. An elephant. Not a cow. An elephant.

Over time, Helen's words consumed Kate's thoughts. Words which cut like knives of varying blades. From the broad blade of a chef's knife, flexible boning blade, serrated bread knives, and on occasion, the meat cleaver—Helen never missed. She cut with such precision that even the small and meaningless had begun to feel like paper cuts. Before long, Kate was covered in cuts. Even before one could heal, another one was delivered—once, twice, three times over.

"Are you okay?" Bruce Lester asked, eyeing her from where he sat as Kate gathered his clothes.

"I'm fine," Kate said without looking at him.

"You don't look fine to me, Kate," he said rather perceptively. "You look like you've got some heavy things rolling around in your head."

"It's nothing," Kate smiled. She pulled out a sweater from the chest of drawers. "Let's get you dressed, shall we?"

"I may be old, but I'm not stupid," he said as he raised his arms for Kate to put his sweater on.

Kate sighed. "It's my mom."

"She still on your case?"

It was ironic to Kate. There she was, caring for other people's parents; bathing them, washing them, making them laugh, and generally being their companions—and yet, she couldn't stand to be with her own mother. "When has she ever stopped?" Kate sniffed. "Anyway, let's not talk about her. We've got lots to do today."

"In case you haven't noticed, I've got plenty of time, Kate," Bruce said. "Why don't you lighten that load you're carrying?"

Kate smiled at Bruce. His wispy, white hair stood on attention. Kate grabbed a comb from the dresser and smoothed his hair down. She relented and eventually told him about her mother. And when he was all dressed, she helped him into his wheelchair and took him out to the garden for a mid-morning stroll. And in all that time, Kate spoke and Bruce listened. She found herself telling him more than she'd expected to.

"It's a tricky one, isn't it?" Bruce said when she'd finished.

It *was* a tricky one. "Hmm, yes, it is," Kate agreed.

"And you find it difficult to stand up for yourself because of your cultural obligations to her as your mother, is that correct?"

"Yes. It just isn't done. Filipino children are supposed to look after their parents in their old age," Kate explained. "And with my dad gone, I'm all she's got. How's she going to survive?"

Bruce opened his mouth to speak; instead, he burst into a coughing fit. He was growing weaker by the day, and Kate didn't like the sound of his cough. She gently rubbed his back and reached for his bottle of water, handing it to him when he finished. "Better?"

Bruce took a sip of water and nodded, a few coughs in between. "The way I see it," Bruce said as he cleared his throat, "you need to put some boundaries in place."

Kate parked the wheelchair next to their favorite bench—the one underneath a Mulberry tree—where they could see all the goings-on. She helped Bruce on to the bench. "So I've been told," she said. "Easier said than done, I'm afraid."

"I'm ninety-one-years-old, Kate, and I like to think I've earned the right to talk about life," Bruce said. He sighed. "Things are not always as important as you young people make them out to be."

Some say that only the good die young; and for a moment, when she was younger and more naïve, Kate believed it. But over the last few years, she had met so many incredible people—young and old alike. Bruce was yet another testimony to the ridiculousness of the old adage. Kate felt instead that age was just a number and that you're only as old as you feel, for with each day that passed, Kate aged—another line of hurt appeared on her face, a wrinkle of frustration, a stain of pain, an additional cut delivered by her mother.

"It's hard to love someone if you can't first love yourself," Bruce continued. "Yes, it is easier said than done, but that is part of loving yourself. It is part of your self-care. People will always treat you the way that you allow them to. And that's true whether that person be your friend, your enemy, or your case, your mother."

Kate didn't say anything. She ran her fingertips along the grass and then looked out into the distance. That was same thing Louise had told her once before. "People will treat you the way you allow them to treat you. This is your life and if you don't live it for yourself, then someone else will."

"It's hard," Bruce said. "Life in itself requires bravery—whatever form that may come in. You will have to find the courage from within yourself to lay those boundaries down. And if she doesn't respect those boundaries, then you'd know she doesn't respect you. And you, my dear, are worthy of love and respect. You taught me that, remember?" Bruce coughed, this time it was wheezy, tired. "Life is too short to live by other people's rules and demands; and you are young for such a fleeting moment. You've got to be smart. Take life by the horns and ride it, come what may. Your mother — she brought you into this world...but it doesn't mean she owns you." Bruce cleared his throat and hacked into a tissue that Kate handed to him. "Kahlil Gibran—do you know him?" Bruce asked Kate.

Kate shook her head.

"He was a poet...a painter, an artist." Bruce's speech was slow and his movements were deliberate, except for the trembling of his jowls as he spoke. "Gibran said, 'Your children are not your children. They are the sons and daughters of Life's longing for itself. They come through you but not from you, and though they are with you, yet they belong not to you.'"

Kate wiped the tears that gathered at the corners of her eyes.

"Always remember that, Kate. Know your worth."

Chapter 38

Louise Delaney

It had been two days since Madison arrived. The moment of shock had pushed Louise into a different world; a world of delirium and paranoia.

"How are you feeling this morning?" Madison asked, handing her a cup of tea.

Louise smiled and gazed at her daughter's face. She looked just like her father. She had the same long black curly hair as Abby's. One couldn't deny their relationship. They shared a parent. "Philip told me what happened," she said. "I'm sorry you had to see that."

Madison shook her head and sat down, placing a teaspoon of sugar and a splash of milk into her own cup. "I'm just glad you're okay now."

Two days. That had been the most that Louise had spent in the other world. The world where she knew no one—or only a precious few. The world where she is a child that needs tending to, that needs to be taught how to do things, or have things done for her. It was a world she knew nothing of, but seemed to keep returning to. "I'm happy that you're home, Madison."

Madison shifted in her seat. She was cautious. Tentative. "Abby told me you were sick."

"Did she?" Louise asked.

Madison nodded. "She reached out to me on Instagram."

A smile formed along the edges of her lips. "She's a good girl." Louise took a sip of her tea, appreciating how the warm liquid flowed down her throat.

"Why didn't you tell me you were sick?"

It was a fair question. Why didn't she tell her? Louise exhaled. "I didn't know how to." Her answer was weak. The truth was, Louise didn't know if Madison would care—whether she had to know, whether she'd want to know.

"And what about Abby? Why didn't you tell me about her?" Madison's tone was both sad and accusatory.

"Would you have wanted to know?" Louise hadn't wanted to taint Madison's perception of her father. He was her hero, the parent who had done no wrong.

Madison pouted, just like when she was a little girl.

"I wasn't sure if I would ever see you again." Louise felt vulnerable as she reached for her daughter's hand.

Madison closed her eyes and took a deep breath. "Tell me about her."

Louise told Madison about her half-sister...how they met, how Abby had run away from home, the encounter with Abby's mother. Her mind was racing, desperate to remember all the details. The mind that she was told she would soon lose was busy ticking away. Louise studied all of Madison's facial expressions. She took them all in, looking out for signs of hurt, anger, betrayal—anything that signaled for Louise to stop talking. But there were none, so she told her everything.

"Are you close to her?" Madison asked.

Louise gazed upon Madison's face. Was there jealousy in her question? Did it hurt her to ask it? Madison had always been a brave child. She was fearless, possibly due to Louise's parenting—or lack of it. It could have gone either way. Madison could have turned into a statistic; a neglected child, raised by the system or worse, the streets. Instead, she'd gone the other way, finding strength within herself, despite being unloved. She'd built walls no one could bring down and pushed herself to the top where she sat with a loving husband and their child. "Yes," Louise said softly.

Madison searched her pockets for something and pulled out a hair-tie. She ran her fingers through her hair and in one swift motion, pulled it together into a bun. Her leg shook furiously underneath the table.

"I'm sorry," Louise said.

Madison waved hand in front of her and shrugged. "Don't be. It wasn't your fault."

The air between them was strained, even awkward. It hurt Louise that she didn't know how to carry a conversation with her own daughter. "I was happy to learn you'd had a daughter." Louise had seen the photos on Facebook, the only window she had into her Madison's life. "What's her name?"

"Eloise," Madison said. "We call her Lulu."

For a brief moment, their eyes connected.

Madison wiped the tears that trickled down her cheek. "I named her after you."

Chapter 39

Abby Delaney

Abby went around the bookstore, dusting the shelves, as well as the tops and spines of the books. Never in her wildest dreams did she ever think she'd be working in a bookstore, much less owning one. When Louise told her she'd transferred the shop to her name, she couldn't believe it. A lawyer was present, and the three of them had signed the paperwork. It was just like she'd seen in the movies.

She'd been both scared and excited. But now that Madison was back, Abby wondered if things would change between her and Louise. Abby felt a pang of jealousy and quickly berated herself for harboring such selfish thoughts.

"What if she, like, loves her daughter more and then kicks me out of the house?" Abby asked Shelby as soon as she returned from her morning break.

"Huh?" Shelby walked to the back of the counter and hung her jacket up.

"Louise! What if she loves Madison more than me and then she decides to kick me out?" Abby had spent too much time with her thoughts that morning, and she'd worked herself into a nervous frenzy.

"She'd sooner kick me out first," Shelby said. "You're her stepdaughter. I'm just some kid from town that nobody likes. You're being paranoid."

"Shelby, I'm being serious!"

"So am I." Shelby put hair up in a ponytail.

"Do you think things are going to change?" Abby bit her nails. The thought of losing Louise scared her. She was already dealing with the fear of losing Louise to Alzheimer's. It was another thing to lose her to Madison.

"Why would it? I mean, Louise loves you. Like seriously, loves you. You should know that by now."

Abby leaned on the counter and rested her chin on her hand. "You know what the worst part is?"

Shelby pulled up a stool and sat on it. "What?"

"Madison is—like—she's so nice. She's super cool and really friendly."

"Duh, I know...we live together." Shelby shifted into a cross-legged position, balancing on top of the stool. "Why's that the worst part?"

"Because I can't hate her or anything. And she's so pretty. I wish I was like her."

"You are exactly like her." Shelby laughed. "The similarities between you two are actually kinda spooky. It's uncanny."

Abby beamed. "You think we look alike?"

"I told you that you guys look like twins, even just from looking at her photos on Instagram," Shelby said. "I'm the one that feels like the odd one out."

"What do you mean? Why?" Abby frowned.

"Well, you guys are all related. And I'm the blue-haired weirdo living in your room."

Since Madison arrived, Shelby had vacated the spare room and moved into Abby's room. Abby didn't mind it though. She'd spent so much time alone when she was younger that she enjoyed having Shelby share a room with her. Abby wrinkled her nose. "You *are* a blue-haired weirdo," Abby said and laughed. "But definitely my favorite blue-haired weirdo!"

"You know of any others? 'Cuz I'd like to meet them." Shelby rolled her eyes. "Actually, I take that back. I don't want to meet them. I hate people."

"Well, you and I can hate the world together, then," Abby said.

"Promise?" Shelby asked, holding her pinky finger up.

The last few months had been difficult for Abby. No sooner had she called Louise, Mom; she was now set to lose her...another mother. Madison's presence intimidated her and made her feel insecure. It brought her back to feeling like she did when she was a little girl; desperately hoping that her parents would choose her. Choose to stay home, choose to read her a bedtime story, choose to hold her in their arms. Louise had her real daughter back. No one would choose their stepdaughter over their real one. Abby linked her pinky with Shelby's. "I promise."

"Sisters," Shelby said.

"Sisters forever," Abby said with a grin.

Chapter 40

Sarah Gardner

It had been 48-hours and Sarah still hadn't seen or heard from Caleb. She'd pleaded with him to come home, admitting that she was wrong. That she missed him and that she'd been selfish. She'd lost her chance.

Down on her knees, she reached for the weeding tool in her garden basket. She needed to clear her mind. Dwelling on what could have been was a dangerous pastime, and the last thing she needed was to go down another rabbit hole.

"Mommy?"

Sarah looked up at Noah. The late afternoon sun glowed behind his handsome face. "What is it, darling?"

"I want to go back to big school," he said. "I want to see my friends again."

Sarah felt a pinch in her chest, and she knew it was time. Tomorrow, she would make an appointment with the specialist and aim to get the treatment that would help her son. It was her responsibility to help him get the best start in life. Adam wasn't there to guide her hand to a decision. It was hers to make. She was his mother. "Okay," she said as she reached for his hand. "We'll get you back to big school."

As Noah ran off to play with Liam and Zoe, Sarah turned her focus on the large bull thistle that threatened her tulips. It wasn't just the garden that needed weeding. Sarah needed to weed her life too—clear it of distractions so that she could focus on what truly needed her focus. Her children, herself, her relationships. She needed to take care of those that mattered.

Her thoughts went to Caleb. *Is Caleb a weed?* she thought to herself. She missed him sorely. Their time apart had made Sarah realize that she'd gotten together with Caleb too soon after Adam's death—even before she'd been able to grieve properly. That was her biggest mistake. But this time, it was different. She knew what losing Caleb meant to her. She now knew who she was without him. Some people never find love in their lifetime, much less twice. Sarah hoped it wasn't too late for them.

THAT NIGHT, AS SARAH was clearing the kitchen, there was a knock on the door.

"I'll get it!" Liam shouted and raced to answer the door.

"Hang on, Liam, please. Wait for me." Sarah washed her hands and grabbed a kitchen towel before following after Liam. Her heart skipped a beat and she gasped when she saw who stood at the doorway.

"Hi Sarah." Caleb stood tall, carrying Liam, whose arms and legs were wrapped tightly around him. He cracked a soft smile. "Liam was just telling me you guys had been busy gardening."

Sarah nodded. She wanted to run and wrap her arms around him too. "It's the weeds...they were getting a bit out of hand," she said. Sarah cleared her throat. "How's Cory—your student?"

"Broken arm," he said. "Hurts like a bugger, but he'll be fine."

"That's good to know." She took a step towards him. "Are you...?" Sarah was too afraid to ask the question, for what if she didn't get the right answer? She glanced at the floor and saw it. His duffle bag; the one he'd packed when he left them...when she asked him to leave.

Caleb nodded. "I'm home," he said.

And just like that, the floodgates opened. Sarah's tears flowed without hesitation.

Noah came out from the kitchen and shrieked. "Caleb!" He raced to Caleb's side and hugged him at the hips.

Caleb put Liam down and lifted Noah high up. "How are you, buddy?" he asked.

"Mommy said I can go back to big school now," Noah beamed.

"Wow! That's great news!" Caleb glanced at Sarah.

Sarah wiped her tears and smiled. "We're going to the specialist," she said. "It's time."

Caleb turned back to Noah. "You're going to have a great time at school, kiddo," he said. "I'm sure your friends will be excited to see you again."

Sarah tightened her grip around the kitchen towel that was still in her hands. Her heart swelled at the sight of her boys all over Caleb, excited, telling him about their day and other stories they'd kept for him.

"Can I just say hi to your mom first?" he asked the kids, setting Noah back down.

"Mommy missed you," Liam said all too knowingly.

Caleb grinned. "Did she?"

Liam nodded.

"Well, I missed her too," Caleb said. "And I missed you guys a lot!"

"Are you staying now?" Noah asked. "Are you?"

"I'm home now, boys," Caleb said as he stepped towards Sarah and cupped her cheek in his hand. He gazed into her eyes and gently planted a soft kiss on her lips, lingering for a brief moment. "I'm home now."

Summer

There is an extremely powerful force that, so far, science has not found a formal explanation to. It is a force that includes and governs all others, and is even behind any phenomenon operating in the universe and has not yet been identified by us. This universal force is love.

~Albert Einstein

Chapter 41

Kate Morgan

Bruce Lester had died in his sleep. Kate had known it was going to happen. It was *always* going to happen. But still, it broke Kate to know that he'd been alone.

"He left me a letter," Kate told Louise that night when she'd visited after her work. "And a book."

"A book?" Louise asked curiously.

"Yes," Kate nodded. She reached into her purse and handed the book to Louise. "*The Prophet.*"

"Ah, yes,"—Louise nodded—"I know the one."

"He had bookmarked a page for me—it's a poem called—"

"*Your Children,*" Louise finished Kate's sentence for her.

"Yes! How did you know?" Kate asked.

"It sounds to me like Bruce Lester was a smart man." Louise took the book from Kate and carefully flipped through the pages, some of which had been dog-eared. "He was considered a rebel of his time, you know?"

Kate shook her head. It was her first introduction to the poet. Poetry was never her thing.

"He was wise beyond his years. A romantic. He believed in both the good in humankind—and the bad," Louise said.

Kate admired the amount of general knowledge that Louise had. Her love for books was amazing. It saddened her to know that one day, all that knowledge would be locked away, never to be accessed again.

"Take his advice," Louise said.

Kate wrinkled her eyebrows. "What advice?"

"Read the poem and then you'll understand." Louise passed the book back to Kate.

Kate ran her fingers over the book. "How are things going with you? You must be so happy that Madison is home."

Louise smiled. She looked tired that day. "I am. It's been a joy having her here. But I have to be realistic and know that she will be leaving soon. She has her family and her life to get back to."

Kate nodded. She couldn't imagine how hard it must be for Louise to let go of her daughter yet again.

"But I'm happy for her. She's a good girl. I just wish I'd been a better mother." Louise's eyes were vacant, almost lifeless, until tears welled up.

Kate reached for her hand, covering it with hers.

"Yesterday," Louise said, "I was cooking an omelet." She looked up at Kate as her tears fell. "But I'd walked away from it. I must have forgotten...I don't know." Louise took a deep breath.

It was the first time that Louise had shown any real emotion about her condition. Kate's heart broke at the sight of Louise's tears.

"A small fire had started," her voice trembled. "Luckily, the fire alarm sounded. Madison was home, so she was able to put it out on time."

Kate gasped, her heart tapping. "I'm so glad nothing happened, and that Madison was home with you at the time."

Louise squeezed her hand. "I'm so scared, Kate," she said, her face filled with dread. "I hardly recognize myself anymore."

Kate pushed her own tears back. "I promise you; it will be okay." It was a promise she'd made to Bruce, too—a promise she could never have kept. "I will be here with you. Every step of the way. I promise you."

Louise shifted in her seat. She opened her mouth to speak and then hesitated.

"What is it?" Kate asked.

Louise shook her head.

"I know you," Kate said. "You were going to say something. What is it?"

Louise folded her hands over her lap and looked into Kate's eyes. "What I'm about to say will hurt, but I want you to know that hurting you is not my intention."

Kate blinked and nodded, unconsciously holding a breath in.

"I cannot keep telling you what you refuse to hear."

Kate opened her mouth to speak when Louise stopped her.

"Please,"—Louise put a hand up—"let me finish."

Kate pressed her lips together and nodded.

"Your life is the most important thing you have. It is a gift, and it is your responsibility to live it. Your mother does not care about you. I have observed how much her toxicity has drained you. And there will come a time, when you have nothing left to give—to her, to Adam, to yourself. I know you want to make her happy, but *her* happiness is her responsibility, just as much as *your* happiness is your own."

Kate looked down at her hands and bit her bottom lip.

"I want to see you happy again, Kate. But only you can do that for yourself. If I could wave a magic wand to make it happen, I would. If hitting you on the head with a fry pan would make you realize just how unbalanced your relationship with your mother is—believe me, I wouldn't hesitate to bring that pan over your head."

Kate laughed.

"Darling, my point is, you've got to take charge of your life. Your mother is fifty-years-old. I heard somewhere that fifty is the new thirty,"—Louise smiled—"so really, there's no reason that she can't manage on her own, especially if she really wanted to. You need to cut the apron strings, darling, and set yourself free. One day, Adam will be a grown man. I don't think for one second that you would do to him what your mother is doing to you."

Kate took a deep breath and let out a long and slow exhale. She never really knew what it meant to cut the apron strings until now. It was time.

Chapter 42

Louise Delaney

Louise hadn't intended on telling Kate just how afraid she was. But things were becoming more obvious—both to her and everyone around her. She was a shadow of her former self.

Madison handed her a cup of tea. "Here you go, Mom," she said. "Can I get you anything else?"

"There's something I need to tell you," she looked up into her daughter's eyes, "before my mind goes completely."

"What is it?" Madison asked.

Madison was always pragmatic. Never one to show her true feelings. *I did that*, thought Louise. *It's my fault she's that way.* Louise tightened her grip on the cup as she felt her hands tremble. "I should have tried harder, Maddie." She hadn't called her that since Madison was ten or eleven years old. "I should have been there for you."

"Mom—"

"Please," Louse said, reaching for her daughter's hand, "I need to say this."

Madison sat by her on the sofa.

"I owe you an apology." Louise looked at her daughter; her beautiful daughter. "I should have been stronger. You needed a mother, and I wasn't there," Louise said. "If I could go back in time..." Louise took a deep breath in. "I'm sorry, Maddie. I am so sorry."

"Mom, I know," Madison said. "You don't need to apologize. I should have been more understanding."

"No." Louise shook her head. "You were a child, and you did not owe me anything—not an ounce of understanding or forgiveness, do you hear me? Your only responsibility was to be a child." Louise recalled the poem of Kahlil Gibran, '*You are the bows from which your children, as living arrows, are sent forth*'.

"It was a difficult time for all of us," Madison said. She wiped her own tears and pushed her hair away from her face.

It was a difficult time. When Amari died, Louise had died with her. She was just an infant. No parent should ever have to bury their own child. It goes against all rules of nature. "I should have been stronger," Louise said.

Madison pressed her lips together. "For a very long time," she said, "I admit, I was angry. And when Dad died, I just felt like I needed to get out of here." Madison wiped her tears once more. "I had many years to get over it—to get over myself—but I chose to be selfish, and I hung on to every feeling of hate and anger that I could muster." She looked away before returning her gaze to Louise. "But I needed someone to blame. I needed someone to blame for the way that I was feeling." Madison blew out a breath. "I used to wonder why I was so unlovable."

Louise sniffed. "You are *so* lovable, Maddie. You deserve to be loved."

"Before I met Scott, I was so afraid of getting close to anyone, because I didn't want to get hurt. I almost lost him. But he persisted and taught me what it felt like to be loved."

Louise took Madison's face in her hands. "You matter and you are loved. You will always be my girl. And I want to spend the rest of my life making sure you know that." Louise looked at her daughter—so beautiful and intelligent. She was in awe of how Madison had ever come out on the other side of such a dark childhood.

"When I had Eloise," Madison continued. "That's when I finally understood. That's when I realized that it wasn't that you didn't love me." Madison wiped her tears with the sleeve of her sweater. "It was that you lost a child that you yet hadn't had time to show your love to." Madison's voice cracked. "I'm so sorry, Mama. I'm so sorry you lost Amari."

"I'm sorry you lost her too, darling. She was your baby sister," Louise said. "We all lost Amari."

"I can't even begin to imagine what you went through." Madison shook her head. "If anything were to ever happen to Eloise…" her voice trailed off.

Louise reached for her Madison. Madison inched closer and Louise held her in her arms, just like when she was a child. She held her the way that she should have held her all those years ago. Louise stroked Madison's hair; Madison, who was now all grown up. "Ssh," she hushed. "It's all going to be okay." Louise closed her eyes and inhaled the scent of the first person who taught her what love truly was.

Chapter 43

Sarah Gardner

"Mommy, where are we going?" Noah asked from the back seat of the car.

"We're going to visit Daddy," Sarah said and glanced at Caleb, who was driving.

"I want to go down," Zoe called from her car seat.

"We're not far now, pumpkin," Sarah replied.

"But I want to go down now," Zoe insisted.

"Kids, huh?" Caleb reached for Sarah's hand and grinned. "Why do want to keep them again?"

Sarah smiled and leaned over, placing her head on his shoulders. It was a beautiful summer's day, and hundreds of hydrangeas lined the streets of Carlton Bay. They drove through a canvas of hues and Sarah couldn't have felt any better than she did that day.

She'd invited everyone for a summer picnic at the cemetery. It was an unusual place for a picnic, but she wanted the children to be around Adam.

Caleb switched his turn signal on and made a left into the Village Cemetery.

"I know this place," Liam exclaimed. "It's Daddy's place!"

"You're right, buddy," Caleb grinned at him in from the rearview mirror. "We're gonna have a picnic with your dad."

"I don't want a picnic!" Zoe said defiantly, her personality growing bolder each day.

"Don't you?" Caleb asked.

"No!" Zoe pouted.

"Oh, well that's a shame. All your friends will be there too. Adam, Abby, Shelby," he listed.

"I want a picnic!" Zoe chirped.

"I thought you might," Caleb said with a laugh.

WHEN THE OTHERS ARRIVED, they joined all their picnic blankets together and carefully laid out the food. Club sandwiches, egg sandwiches, pastries, carrot sticks with sour cream and chive dip, apples and bananas—it was impressive.

"Wow!" Kate beamed. "We have enough to feed a small army."

"Have you seen our army?" Sarah joked as she motioned to the lot of them.

"What a gorgeous day for a picnic." Louise took a deep breath and looked up at the sky. "It's absolutely stunning!"

"Where do we sit?" Helen asked.

"Anywhere you feel like," Sarah gestured around her. Helen frowned, but Sarah did not let it get to her. Nothing was going to rattle her today.

"Philip," Sarah called out to him as she gathered the children around the picnic.

Philip who had been talking to Shelby turned to look at Sarah.

"Would you lead us in prayer before we eat, please, Philip?"

He smiled. "Absolutely!" Philip jogged towards the group and once the children settled, he began. "Almighty Father, we thank you for bringing us together on this beautiful day as we sit amongst our loved ones. We thank you for the bounty that you have blessed us with."

Sarah looked up from prayer, and her heart overflowed with gratitude and love. She glanced at Caleb, who was sat next to her with both Zoe and Noah on his lap. And then she looked at all her friends who had become her family.

"Heavenly Father, we pray for our friends and family. Only you know the deep longing that lives in their hearts." Philip paused and opened his eyes. He looked at Sarah from across the circle and nodded.

Sarah took a deep breath and smiled. She turned to Caleb. "Caleb," she said. "from the moment you came into my life, my heart knew that you would heal me and make me whole again."

Caleb's lips formed a smile as he held her hand in his.

"It was in sadness that you came into our home. And since then, you had turned that sadness into joy." Sarah's voice quivered. "I know I'm a little bit loony," she said with a laugh. "And I can be a handful too."

"Yup," Caleb joked and grinned.

"You inspire me to be a better person," Sarah continued, "a better mom, and a better friend." She glanced at Kate and Louise and instantly, she could feel the tears in the back of her throat.

"Go on," Kate whispered, encouraging her.

"Caleb," Sarah looked from Caleb and down at her hands. She twisted her wedding ring off her finger and placed it gently insider her purse. And then she pulled out a small blue box and looked back up at Caleb. "Thank you for not giving up on me and the children," she said.

Sarah pushed herself off the ground and onto one knee. She heard Abby and Shelby whispering excitedly and smiled. Taking a deep breath, she asked, "Caleb Myers, our story is just beginning. Will you do me the honor and write the rest of it with me?" Sarah opened the box and in it was a simple gold band. "I don't want to wake up another day without you by my side."

"Wow...I never thought I'd be the one getting a proposal," Caleb said with a laugh, prompting everyone to laugh with him. "But hey, I'm not complaining. Come here, you," he said as he pulled Sarah into a soft, loving kiss.

"Is that a yes?" Sarah asked.

"Oh you bet it is!" Caleb grinned. And with that, everyone cheered and called out congratulatory wishes.

Philip raised a hand to remind everyone that they were still in prayer. "And now, Heavenly Father, we ask that you lay your great hands upon Sarah and Caleb. May you bless them always and guide them with your love. In you alone forever, oh Lord. Amen."

"Amen!" Everyone cheered and clapped once more, hugging those next to them.

Chapter 44

Kate Morgan

Kate was delighted for Sarah. She knew how hard things had been for Sarah and she was happy that her friend had found someone that she could trust and share her life with.

"Didn't her husband just die?" Helen whispered loudly to Kate.

Kate closed her eyes and took a deep breath in. "Please, don't start now, Ma."

"I'm just saying. It's hardly appropriate that she's marrying so soon after her husband had died. And why would anyone propose in a cemetery? It's just so morbid! And next to her dead husband's grave!"

"We should all be so lucky," Kate whispered sharply. "She's happy, and that's all that matters to me."

"It's called values, Katherine. Some of us clearly have none."

Honor thy father and thy mother, Kate chanted in her head.

"And what is it with that Shelby? How can you expose your son to someone like that?" Helen spat. "It is disrespectful to God. And to think there is a priest here."

"Hi Helen." Philip sat down next to Helen.

"Oh, Father, hi," Helen smiled graciously. "That was a lovely prayer. Did you know about the proposal?"

Philip nodded. "I did. Sarah told me her plans and asked that I join them in prayer."

"Interesting," Helen said.

"Do you think so?" Philip asked.

Helen cocked her head to the side. "It's just unusual, don't you think? Her husband had just died. I think four years is much too soon."

"They have been gifted with a chance at happiness together," Philip said. "I think of it more as a blessing."

"Father, what about that boy—or girl, whatever," Helen motioned towards Shelby who was playing tag with the children. "That girl is living in sin and she's spreading her wrong values to the children."

Kate closed her eyes tight. She was unnerved, embarrassed, and truthfully, just angry and over it. "Philip," she said in a low voice, "I'm so sorry."

Philip smiled. "There's no need to be sorry, Kate." Turning to Helen, he said, "God loves everyone."

"But she's living in sin!" Helen's face was peppered with disgust. "What if they're having a relationship? She's a bad influence on a young girl like Abby."

"They're friends," Philip said. "I suggest that we do not put them in a box or add to any pressures either one of them are already living with. Why don't we just love them—both of them—for who they are?"

Helen sneered and shrugged her shoulders.

"Einstein once said, '*There is an extremely powerful force that, so far, science has not found a formal explanation to. It is a force that includes and governs all others. This universal force is love.*'" Philip paused. "He said, '*Love is light, that enlightens those who give and receive it. Love is gravity, because it makes some people feel attracted to others. Love is power, because it multiplies the best we have, and allows humanity not to be extinguished in their blind selfishness. Love unfolds and reveals. For love, we live and die. Love is God and God is Love.*'"

Kate glanced at her mother, who had grown silent.

Philip continued. "Jesus founded his kingdom in love and now, there are over 2.5 billion people who would die for him. I am one of them." He placed a hand on Helen's shoulder. "Love them as individuals. Let Shelby know that she is loved. Let her work through her identity in her own time. Pressure is not helpful to anyone, especially not to one as young as Shelby."

"Well, it certainly doesn't help that Louise condones their behavior," Helen said.

"It is always easier to deal with an issue when that issue is not in your own home. Everyone has their own thing that they are working on." Philip was calm. He didn't preach or push. He only spoke the truth.

"Why don't you tell her? Tell Abby that Shelby is a bad influence on her. I'm sure she will listen to you." Helen pushed.

"God did not call me to judge people. He asked me to love them," he said. "God will help them through their issues, as he will help you with yours."

Kate knew it was time. It was time to cut the strings. "Mother—that's enough. It's one thing for you to constantly put me down, but I will not have you say such things about my friends."

Helen laughed. "Your friends?"

"I'm not done speaking," Kate said. Her heart was racing. It banged against her chest so wildly that she thought it would burst. But it was a long time coming. "I've put up with your insults. I have tried to make you happy. I have tried to please you and nothing I do ever seems to be enough. I cannot do this anymore." Kate shook her head. "No—I will not do this anymore. If you hate it here so much—if you hate *me* so much, if you think that I'm such a disappointment, then by all means, go home. Go back to the Philippines. Because this is *my* life. This is *my* home. These are *my* friends."

"My goodness, Katherine, can't you take a joke?" Helen laughed and put a hand on Kate's arm. "Where's your sense of humor?"

But Kate wasn't having it. She snatched her arm away.

"Well, I'm sorry if offended you," Helen said. "I'm *eternally* grateful for what you have done in the past. You've done more than you should, and I'm proud of you—more than you will ever be proud of yourself."

There it was again. Helen always did that. She always turned things around at any sign of Kate standing up against her.

"I am alive and well because of you and your ability to help, and I thank God I raised a financially capable child. Thank you for all that you've done. I mean it. *Much gratitude*," Helen said. She mastered the fine art of passive aggression.

Kate cringed at every spoken word.

"After all, isn't that what families are for? Don't you re-member all the other things that *I've* done for you? That your father has done for you?" And there it was. The verbal slaps. One—slap, two—slap, three—slap.

"You always do this. You always do this to me. Every time I try to stand up for myself, you dig things up from the past. Well, you know what? I'm done! I'm not doing this with you any longer."

"Well, it's because your memories are somewhat made up and twisted, in my opinion. I can't let you go on doing that to me and more importantly, to yourself."

Kate's head was spinning. Were all her memories twisted? Made up? She looked around her. Everyone was busy doing their own things; but Kate saw Louise glance her way.

"You seem to have conveniently forgotten everything *I've* done for you," Helen said. "But look, I don't want to fight. I merely wish to be able to say what I need to say. I'm your moth-er...if that's still meaningful to you in any way. I think that's a small ask from the person that almost died giving birth to you."

Kate narrowed her eyes at her mother. She shook her head. What was going on? "What the—"

"The absence of your father does not give you the right to dishonor me—to tell me to go back to the Philippines. How dare you!" Helen's eyes bore into Kate's. Saliva gathered at the corners of her mouth the way that it did every time Helen turned her cruel streak on. It was like *Dr. Jekyll* and *Mr. Hyde*. "I understand you're a grown woman now. Having said that, how-ever, I'm still your mother and I'll be damned if I let you talk to me like that. Honor thy father and thy mother. That's the fourth commandment, in case you've forgotten your Catholic faith. In fact, you don't even have to be Catholic to adhere to that commandment. All it takes is plan common sense, common decency," Helen spat. "I never would have treated my mother this way, albeit the cruel and tyrannical way she and my father treated me."

Kate couldn't breathe. The words were caught in her throat. Her mother was winning again; circling around her, intimidating her. First, a blow to the ribs, then a hook to the jaw. The boxing bell was going to ring any minute now.

"Was I really so evil that you would treat me this way in front of your friends, Katherine? We had the best of relationships, don't you remember? I only ever wanted to give you what I never had—a *good* mother."

Kate ran a hand through her hair. "I've failed the test again, haven't I?" She shook her head, frustrated and angry. "I'm not retaking it. No more. I'm out."

"There was never a test. Don't be so melodramatic," Helen said. And there it was, the finishing uppercut followed by the ding of the boxing bell.

"I mean, I've failed you as a daughter. I'm done trying. It's time for you to go," Kate said.

Helen held her chin up, looked at Philip and then back at Kate. "I'm a bit tired now. Would you mind taking me home?"

Kate opened her mouth to speak when Philip said, "You stay, Kate. I'll be happy to drive Helen home. That is, if that's alright with you, Helen?"

Helen nodded. "Thank you," she said.

And just like that, the match had ended.

After Helen and Philip left, Kate wandered away from the group. She needed a moment to breathe, to gather herself and her emotions. She looked at her hands, still trembling from the encounter; the hands that finally cut the apron strings. *No more. I'm out.* The words played in her head. *I've failed you as a daughter. I'm done trying. It's time for you to go.*

Did Kate win? Or did Helen?

Were the apron strings cut off?

Kate furiously wiped her tears. She thought the snip to freedom would have made her ecstatic; instead, she was overwhelmed with emotions—anger, regret, guilt. Kate was embittered. Her triumphant win in the fight ring made her feel empty. Perhaps it was she who had lost the match.

Kate felt a hand on her shoulder. "Darling, are you okay?" It was Louise.

"That didn't look very pleasant," Sarah said.

Kate wiped her nose with the back of her hand. "I'm sorry, Sarah," she said. "I didn't mean to cause such a drama on your special day."

"Hey..." Sarah's voice was soothing. "Come here." Sarah pulled Kate into an embrace.

Kate fell into Sarah's arms and sobbed. Hot tears fell from her eyes as she choked on her cries. Unable to hold it in any longer, Kate let herself be vulnerable and wept into Sarah's embrace.

"You just let it out, darling," Kate heard Louise say. "Everything you're feeling; just let it all out."

For the first time in years, Kate let her emotions go. The inhibitions that had held her back slipped out with every tear and every sob; the chains of tradition slowly breaking away.

It was neither momentous nor triumphant.

It would take a while before Kate could come to terms with her freedom; for before that, she would need to recover, to heal the wounds, the cuts, and the bruises.

THAT NIGHT, AS KATE parked up the driveway, she turned to look in the backseat. Adam was fast asleep. He was her pride, her joy, her love. Kate rubbed her weary eyes before she slowly opened the door and unbuckled the car seat to carry him in.

"Is he asleep?"

Kate nearly jumped. She hadn't expected Helen to be in the living room. The last time they'd argued, Helen had barricaded herself in her bedroom—pushing the bed against the door, the dresser, and everything else that wasn't bound to the floor. But that night, Helen sat on the sofa, calm...perhaps even timid and meek. Kate nodded. "I'll take him up to his room and put him to bed."

When she went back down, Helen was waiting for her.

"Kate, can we talk?" Helen asked.

Kate studied her mother. "I'm really not in the mood to talk about people living in sin, or how I could do better as a mother, or even how I need to watch what I eat because I will never be happy being fat," she said.

"Kate, please."

Kate sighed, exhausted. "I'm going to make a cup of tea. Do you want one?"

Helen nodded and followed her into the kitchen.

As they sat down with their cups of tea, silence hung heavily between them. "Kate," Helen began. "I'm sorry."

Kate scoffed. She didn't want to say it was okay; or that it would be better in the morning; or that they should just forget about it and move on. Because it wasn't okay. It wasn't going to be better in the morning. And she certainly could not just forget it and move on. Kate had grown used to her mother throwing words out and then apologizing after the damage had been done. While it would have been easier to accept the apology and move on, Kate decided she was done. *Life is too short to live by other people's rules and demands; and you are young for such a fleeting moment. You've got to be smart. Take life by the horns and ride it, come what may.* Bruce Lester's words rang through her head. It was time for Kate to live her life...come what may.

"I'm sorry," Helen said once more. "I've been a poor mother to you. You deserved better. You still deserve better."

Kate looked up from her cup and into her mother's eyes. For the first time since Kate had known her mother, Helen was calm, her face defeated. Kate quickly looked away.

"I—there are so many things that I should have done differently." Helen clasped her hands around the cup of tea. "I should have let you be your own self. Instead, I pressed and pushed. I was controlling, abusive with my words, and Kate," she choked, "for what it's worth, I am sorry."

Kate clenched her jaw and swallowed as she tried to hold her tears back. She didn't want her mother to see her cry; to give her the satisfaction in knowing that she had succeeded in breaking her.

"I never felt love—not from my parents or siblings," Helen said.

Kate had heard the story many times. Helen's parents were abusive, especially her mother. Her father never did anything to protect Helen or her siblings. He whipped out his belt when her mother asked him to, and he hit them when she told him to. That was why Kate's parents never took her to see her grandparents. They moved across to the other end of the island to get away from them. Helen had always talked about how she had protected Kate from her own parents, as if Kate owed her for the respite from abusive grandparents.

"I said that I would never be like her." Helen wiped her tears. "I swore that I would never do what they did to me. I tried," Helen said, "but it was the only kind of love I'd ever known."

Kate wanted her to stop. It was always the same excuse. At one point, Kate considered Helen her best friend. They talked about anything and everything. And then when she left for the United States, everything had changed. Kate wondered if any of it had been real—both the friendship and the abuse. Helen had accused her of having twisted memories. Did she? Were her memories twisted? Had she romanticized the past? Or did she turn it into some psychological thriller? She didn't want to hear any more. "Look..."

Helen raised a hand, telling Kate to stop. Kate pursed her lips and closed her eyes so her mother wouldn't see her rolling them.

"Your father,"—Helen blew out a breath—"he didn't die of a heart attack." Helen let out a loud sob that sent shivers down Kate's spine.

Kate looked up, confused. She gritted her teeth. "What do you mean he didn't die of a heart attack?"

Helen looked away and wiped her tears. "He took his own life," she said softly. "He..." Helen broke down, her words turned into sobs that rendered her incoherent.

She'd never seen her mother cry. Not like this. Tears fell from her eyes, flowing as if from an endless stream. Her cries bordered on hysterical blubbering. Kate wanted to reach out, to touch her mother, to comfort her. But she couldn't for every time she raised her own hand, it trembled violently.

"It was my fault," Helen cried. "I pushed him, kicked him when he was down. He lost his job, and I admonished him for it. I'm so ashamed of myself. I'm a terrible mother and I was a horrible wife. I never deserved either of you. Not you, and most certainly not your father." Helen bowed her head in her hands, her shoulders shaking with each sob.

So many questions raced around Kate's mind. So many questions she'd wanted to ask—but she didn't. *"God did not call me to judge people,"* she heard Philip's words in her head. *He asked me to love them. God will help them through their issues, as he will help you with yours."*

Kate's heart hurt. What did it mean that her father took his life? Was he depressed? Did he seek help for his depression? Her heart ached for her father, who knew no other way out of the darkness he must have been feeling, and for her mother, who carried the heavy weight of guilt and blame.

Kate let her tears fall and together, mother and daughter cried tears for the past that; the past that weighed more than they could carry.

Finally, Kate reached for her mother's hands and held them in hers—not for Helen's sake, but for her own.

"I'm going back home," Helen said. "To the Philippines. Philip helped me get a ticket this afternoon. The flight leaves tomorrow."

"What? Why?" Kate asked, shocked at her mother's announcement.

"I don't belong here, Kate," Helen said. "This is your life. And I too have mine to live."

"But how? I mean, where did you get the money to pay for it?"

Helen avoided Kate's eyes and cast her own down to her guilty hands. "You father left me some money."

Kate couldn't believe what she was hearing. She slowly pulled her hands away. All that time, she'd been working, getting as many shifts as she could, missing out on precious time with Adam, just so she could afford to pay for the extra expenses her mother's presence incurred. All that time, Helen had some money. There were so many questions that needed answers.

But it didn't end there. Helen had more to say, more to confess. "He left you some money too." Helen looked away, her lips trembling. "Earlier today, I transferred it into your bank account. Everything he left you, I put it into your account."

Kate could not understand what she was feeling. Was she upset? Angry? Did she feel sorry for her mother? The constant betrayal and manipulation—it was too much.

"Kate," Helen took her only daughter's hands, "he was very proud of you."

Kate looked into her mother's eyes.

"Your father was incredibly proud of you. On the day you left the Philippines," Helen continued, "he said you were so brave; that you had a courageous heart."

Tears fell. Kate had always felt she was a disappointment to her parents. Not once had they told her they were proud of her.

"He was so proud of how you'd followed your heart, no matter the consequences."

Kate covered her face with her hands and sobbed as her mother said the words she'd always longed to hear.

"And I'm proud of you too, Kate." Helen reached for Kate's cheeks and wiped them with her thumbs. "I could only wish to have been able to do the things you've done; the things you've achieved. Don't be like me." Helen shook her head. "Don't wait for the day you wake and realize that you're fifty-years-old with nothing to show for it because you weren't brave enough to live the life you dreamed about."

Kate could not stop her tears. Tears of hope, desperation, and anger fell from her eyes.

"I don't belong here," Helen said. "This is your life, *anak*, not mine."

Anak. Child. Daughter. Kate had never felt like her mother's daughter. She'd been a friend, a confidant. A teacher, an enemy. But that night, for the first time in her life, Kate saw Helen as a *mother*. "I don't understand," Kate said. She wiped her face. Her nose was blocked and her eyes stung. "Was it something Philip had said? What did he say to you?"

Helen shook her head. "No matter how hard we try, one way or another, we will cause our children pain or hurt." Helen smoothed Kate's cheek. "I've caused you more pain, more hurt, than I'd ever imagined. And I'd like the chance to change that, late as it may be."

Helen's face softened. It was not the one that Kate had known. She may never know what Helen and Philip talked about that day; and truth be told, Kate was afraid to find out. She didn't want to find out.

As Kate embraced her mother, it felt—for the first time in her life—that behind all the pain of the past, there was hope for a future.

Chapter 45

Louise Delaney

Louise sat on the sofa with Abby next to her. "Now, from there, you're going to yarn over and pull it through the stitch." She glanced at Shelby who sat on the floor, focused on knitting a hat for Madison's daughter.

She'd been trying to teach them to knit, and while Shelby took to it like a duck to water, Abby struggled. She suggested Abby try crocheting, which she now seemed to be getting the hang of.

Madison sat on the armchair with her legs hanging over one side, just like she did when she was a child. At the sound of a knock on the door, she sat up. "I'll get it!" Madison said as she quickly jumped up.

"It might be Philip. He said he was on his way," Louise said. Turning her attention back to Abby, "Good! That's good! Now, go ahead and do a single crochet on each stitch."

"This is so much better than knitting," Abby said with a grin.

"You're doing very well," Louise said. "And Shelby, looks like you're going to finish that blanket in no time at all."

Louise smiled to herself. Life was good. In the last few weeks, Madison had taken the lead and reached out to the younger girls. Abby and Shelby looked up to her and enjoyed every moment they could get with Madison. Louise glanced at her girls and a warmth filled her heart and she glowed from within. She had *three* beautiful *daughters* and her life couldn't be fuller.

"Mom?" Madison said.

Louise looked up to find Madison carrying a little girl. Her husband, Scott, stood behind her. She gasped and covered her mouth. Before she could utter a word, tears came streaming fast down her face.

Abby and Shelby looked up. "Is that her? Is that Eloise?" Abby got up and fussed over the child.

"Man, she's got tiny feet!" Shelby said as she pushed herself off the floor.

Louise got up and half-jumped-skipped-and-hobbled towards them. She took Scott in a big embrace. "Hello, darling," she said and held him by the shoulders. "You look good. You look really good." Tears filled her eyes.

"Hi Mom," Scott said, returning his mother-in-law's embrace.

Louise turned back to Madison, tears blurring her vision. "You must be Eloise," she said softly but with much excitement. "Hi darling girl, hi." Louise kissed Eloise on both cheeks. Louise wiped her tears with the back of her hand. She held her hands out. "May I?" she asked Madison.

"Lulu," Madison said, "this is your Nana Louise."

"Nana Lulu!" Eloise exclaimed.

"Well, I do love the sound of that voice!" Louise couldn't stop smiling even if she'd tried to. "That's right, sweet pea, I'm your Nana Louise."

"Nana Lulu!" Eloise said again and threw her head back, laughing.

"She knows all about you," Madison said. "Don't you, Lu-lu?"

Louise held Lulu in her arms and kissed the top of her head. She inhaled the scent that only children had—purity, innocence, tenderness. She couldn't believe it. "How did—when—" It was almost overwhelming.

"We arrived today," Scott said. "Madison called us and told us to come."

Louise looked at Madison, who'd nodded. "They were just waiting for my call to get on the plane," Madison said.

"My turn!" Abby piped up.

Madison took Lulu from Louise. "Lulu, this is your Aunty Abby. She's Mommy's little sister."

Abby's eyes widened in surprise. And instead of hugging Lu-lu, as one might have expected, she wrapped her arms around Madison. "Am I really your sister?" Abby sobbed and buried her face in between Madison and Lulu.

"Of course, you are, silly goose," Madison laughed and put an arm around Abby. She turned to Shelby.

"Silly goose!" Lulu squealed and threw her head back again, laughing.

"And this is your Aunty Shelby."

"Shelby!" Lulu parroted, and they all laughed.

"You're just a little parrot, aren't you?" Shelby said.

"I'm a little parrot!" Lulu had put on a show for them, and it was delightful.

That night was the happiest that Louise had been since—she couldn't remember. It was more than she'd ever hoped for. She wished that she could place all her memories into a jar and seal it; opening it on days when she needed them.

Six months later

Kate Morgan

Kate said as she set down a tray of hot cups of tea for the girls. She'd invited Sarah and Louise over for the afternoon. The sky was bright with just a bit of a chill in the air. "I got a text message from Abby this morning," Kate said to Louise. "She said she's coming back tomorrow, is that right?"

"Mmm, yes," Louise said. "I'll serve the tea," Louise said. Over the last few months, Kate had noticed a moderate but obvious decline in Louise's mental state. Conversations had begun to lack substance, and more moments of forgetfulness had taken over.

"How's she doing?" Sarah asked. "Everything okay with her mom?"

Louise nodded. "Yes, she said that she went out to dinner with Rachel and her partner. Abby says Rachel's going well with her recovery. She's off the drugs and alcohol. And she's been dating a minister—can you believe it?"

"Wow..." Kate said, almost sighing. "A minister. I remember when we first met her—she was quite intimidating." She shook her head. "A minister...I can't picture her with a minister."

"That's actually quite nice, isn't it?" Sarah picked up her tea and took a sip. "How does Abby feel about all of it?"

"She's a smart girl," Louise said. "She's taking things slowly. She and Philip had been talking about her feelings—a lot of anger towards Rachel."

"I can understand that," Kate said. After everything she'd been through with her own mother, she had a fair clue of how Abby must have been feeling. "She's so brave for even taking the trip in the first place."

"Shelby had a lot to do with it," Louise said. "The two of them—Abby and Shelby—they really push each other; cheer each other on. It's very comforting for me to know that Abby has that kind of friendship. Kinda like ours," Louise said with a smile. "I can't wait to see her tomorrow. I've really missed her."

"Well, I'm sure she's looking forward to coming home," Sarah said.

"That's exactly what she said in her message." Kate laughed. "Hang on, I'll be right back,"

"Anything I can help with?" Sarah asked.

"See that covered table over there?" Kate pointed to the left of Sarah. "If you could take the sheet off, that would be great."

Kate disappeared into the house and went to the garage. She picked up the three pairs of gloves she bought from the general store just the weekend before and a small bucket of pre-mixed white grout. And lastly, she picked up a black shoebox that sat on the shelf by the door.

"Okay," Kate said as she returned to the garden where Sarah and Louise were chatting animatedly. "I've got something I'd really love for us to work on together."

"Oh! What is it?" Sarah set her cup down and sat upright.

"Today, we'll be doing a bit of craft work," Kate beamed and handed the gloves out to them. "Here—put these on."

"I love arts and crafts," Louise said. "What are we making?"

"Here,"—Sarah said after she'd noticed that Louise was struggling to put the gloves on—"let me help you with those."

Louise looked up at Sarah and patted her cheek. "Thank you, darling."

Kate sat down with the shoebox in front of her. "Do you remember when I broke the hall mirror just over a year ago?"

Sarah groaned. "Do we ever?" she laughed.

"The one that you said would bring you seven years of bad luck?" Louise asked tentatively.

"Yes!" Kate beamed. She could see in Louise's face just how happy she was to have remembered that bit of the past. "I have here,"—she gestured towards the box—"all of those broken pieces."

Sarah made a face. "Why? I would have thought you'd have thrown them out."

"I couldn't,"—Kate sighed—"don't ask me why, but I was too scared to throw them out." Kate uncovered the box. "Anyway, last weekend, I got some supplies. I was hoping that the three of us could craft these broken pieces into something beautiful."

"Someone once said that '*art is making something out of nothing*.'" Louise mused. "I think it will be an interesting activity."

"I also managed to get that old garden table from the thrift store on Lighthouse Road." Kate got up and to show them her purchase.

"Yeah, I know the one," Sarah said of the thrift store. "They've got lots of treasures there. Sometimes, it's really worth being patient and looking through everything they've got. You just never know what you might find."

"When I went in, I really wasn't sure what I was looking for—until I found it," Kate said with a smile. "It's a little bit like you girls. I never realized how lonely I was until I met the two of you."

Sarah scrunched her eyebrows together and smiled. "Aww...Kate, that's so sweet!"

"I mean it," Kate said. "You two—and Adam, naturally—are the best things to ever happen in my life. Not Evan, not Mark...it's you two." Kate reached for both their hands and squeezed them.

"Oh,"—Louise took her hand and wiped her eyes—"you're making me cry!"

Sarah laughed. "Me too!"

"I'm done with men—for now, at least," Kate said with a laugh. "For a very long time, I've lived my life according to what everyone else wanted. I realized, after my mom left, that I really have no idea who I am. I've always been someone's daughter, someone's wife, or girlfriend. And then Adam's mom. But I have no idea who *I* am. So, this year, I want to focus on myself."

"Well, good for you!" Louise cheered her on. "Have you spoken to Helen?" she asked.

Kate nodded. "She emails me most days. She's gone to a doctor, and she's now seeing a therapist."

"Oh, wow..." Sarah leaned back in her chair. "That's really good to know."

"It's a really big step for her. Psychiatry isn't as widely accepted in the Philippines as it is in the States," Kate explained. "I think it's been really helpful for her. They've got a lot of ground to cover, but Mom knows that she needs to take things one day at a time."

"That's very brave of Helen," Louise said. "You should be proud of her."

"I am," Kate said. "It's a shame that it took so much for all of it to come out. But in the end, I think it's for the best."

"You know, I've been thinking...after everything that we've all been through this past year. Life is like a garden," Sarah said. "There are flowers and there are weeds."

"Ah, yes," Louise said. "But weeds are only weeds if you don't want them around."

"That's true," Sarah said. "Sometimes, when life gets prickly, it feels like our garden is overcome with weeds and we feel ourselves suffocating."

"I know the feeling," Kate laughed.

"You know how they say that the grass is always greener on the other side?" Louise asked. "Well, it doesn't mean that weeds don't grow there too."

"Well, gosh, aren't we the philosophical gardeners?" Kate joked, and they laughed together.

"Right, so let's get working on this table," Louise said excitedly

"Wait!" Kate said.

"What is it?" Sarah asked.

Kate picked up her handbag. "See this?"

"Your purse?" Louise asked.

Kate nodded. She placed her bag on the ground and smiled.

"Oooh, purse on the floor," Sarah teased, knowing well how superstitious Kate was. "What gives?" she asked, grinning.

Kate never used to put her bag on the floor. Like many Filipinos, Kate believed the purse to be a symbol of one's wealth and adhered to the superstition that putting your purse on the floor meant 'money out the door'. "I'm done with superstitions," she said, slapping her hands together as it washing it. "Life is too short to be superstitious."

"Hear, hear!" Louise clapped for her friend.

"I'm so proud of you," Sarah said.

"I'm proud of me too," Kate grinned.

"Hey, Kate?" Evan came out to the backyard with Adam in his arms.

Kate turned at the sound of her name. "Oh, hey! Are you boys all set?"

Evan nodded. "We wanted to give Mommy a kiss before we go—don't we, Adam?" Evan leaned over, bringing Adam close enough to Kate for her to kiss.

"Oh my, aren't we just the handsomest boy today?" Louise said.

Kate nuzzled Adam and planted smoochy kisses on his soft cheeks. "I love you, my little man," she said. "You have fun with Daddy today."

"Can I get a kiss too?" Sarah asked as she got up to give Adam a little peck on his chubby cheek.

Adam wriggled restlessly in Evan's arms, eager to get on with the day's adventure. "Someone's excited," Evan said with a grin.

"You boys have fun," Kate said.

"See you later," Evan said as he leaned in and gave Kate a small kiss on the cheek. Then he turned to Sarah and Louise. "You ladies enjoy your afternoon, now, won't you?"

After they left, Sarah turned to Kate. "What was *that*?"

"I agree—what just happened then?" Louise asked.

Kate made a face. "What do you mean?"

"We mean—what's going on between you and Evan?" Sarah leaned forward, resting her elbows on the table.

Kate shook her head. "Nothing. We're just trying to co-parent."

"Uh-uh," Louise wagged a finger at her. "That looked like more than *'we're just trying to co-parent.'*"

"Fine," Kate said. "Evan asked if we could give things another go."

Sarah's eyes widened. "Things...as in?"

"As in—between the two of us," Kate replied.

"What did you say?" Louise asked.

Kate sighed. "I said I wasn't ready for anything right now. I told him what I told you both—that I want to focus on myself first; get to know who I am."

"And? What did he say?" Sarah asked impatiently.

"He said he understood and that he would wait for me." Kate shrugged and took a sip of her tea.

"Well...that's a very mature response on both your parts," Louise said.

"One day at a time," Sarah said. "Good idea."

Kate wasn't sure about where things were between her and Evan. They had, at one point, been crazy in love with each other. When and how things changed, she couldn't quite put a date on it. Since they'd separated—and later divorced—Evan had stopped drinking alcohol and signed himself up with AA. It had been over two years since he'd been dry and Kate was proud of him. But she wasn't looking for a relationship. Not yet. She needed to first build a healthy relationship with herself. "Oh! Did I tell you guys that I bumped into Mark last week?"

"No," Louise frowned, "I don't think so."

"When was that?" Sarah asked.

Kate told them about how Mark was dropping off a delivery at the retirement village just as she was arriving for her shift at work. Though awkward at first, Kate told him about how her mom had gone back to the Philippines and how Helen had told her the truth about her father's death. "I apologized for how things ended between us—you know, how I was too scared to stand up for myself."

"What did he say?" Louise asked.

"He said it was water under the bridge and that he too was sorry that he walked out that night." Kate shrugged. "In the end, we agreed to be friends."

"Aww...poor Mark," Sarah said.

"All things happen for a reason," Louise reminded them.

"Enough about me," Kate said. "How's Noah doing now that he's back in school?" she asked Sarah.

"He's doing so well, you guys," Sarah said, as she beamed like a proud Mama Bear. "He's even going to be in the school play next fall."

"Is he? That's wonderful!" Louise exclaimed.

Sarah nodded. "He's going to be the white rabbit in *Alice in Wonderland*."

Kate laughed. "That's so cute!"

"You should see him at home," Sarah said. "*I'm late, I'm late! For a very important date!*"

"He's the perfect Mr. Rabbit," Louise said. "I can't wait to watch him in action."

"Me too!" Kate said. "I'm going to be cheering so loudly for him—just you wait!"

"Any wedding plans yet?" Louise asked Sarah.

"We've set a date," Sarah said, her smile from ear to ear. "We're hoping for a Spring Wedding next year."

"Eeek! That's so exciting!" Kate cheered.

"And I want you both to be my maids-of-honor," Sarah smiled.

"Well, then we should get started with the planning then," Louise said. "No time to waste."

"This is going to be my first time as a maid-of-honor. I've never even been a bridesmaid. I'm so excited!" Kate said. "Look at us..." Kate mused and sighed. "I love you guys so much."

"How about we get started on that project of yours, Kate?" Louise reminded them.

"Oh, yes! I totally forgot about that," Kate said, laughing.

"And here I thought it was me who was supposed to be the forgetful one," Louise joked.

KATE, SARAH, AND LOUISE began gluing the broken mirror pieces on. One by one, piece by piece, they talked about life and the moments they'd seen each other through.

"I wish," Kate said as she glued a piece on, "to be brave. To be the best version of myself—fearless and confident."

"You're on your way," Sarah said.

"What do you wish for?" Kate asked Sarah.

Sarah twisted her mouth as she glued her last piece in place. "Hmmm,"—she thought—"my wish is to continue to learn to find joy in the present, be grateful for the past, and look forward to the future." Sarah turned to Louise. "What about you, Louise?"

Louise concentrated on the piece of mirror she'd glued on, shifting it ever so slightly. "I've already got my wish," she mumbled.

"What's that?" Kate asked.

Louise looked up from the table. "What's what?" she frowned.

"What was your wish?" Kate clarified.

"Do I have to make a wish?" Louise appeared confused.

Kate felt a small pang in her chest. She smiled at Louise. "We're making wishes," she said to Louise. "What do you wish for?"

Louise paused to think about the question. "I wish for my daughter and her family to come home so I can see them one last time."

Madison, Scott, and Lulu had been living in Carlton Bay for six months now. Madison didn't want to leave her mother, and with Scott working as a program developer, it was easy for him to relocate and continue his work online. "Honey, they're already home, remember?" Kate placed a hand on Louise's back. "Your family *is* home."

It took but a brief moment for it to register. "Yes, yes," Louise said. "That's right. Yes, they are home. You're quite right," she nodded, her movements shaky. And then, as if hit by a moment of clarity, Louise looked up at Kate and then glanced at Sarah. "Then I'd like to make another wish."

"What's that?" Sarah asked encouragingly.

Louise looked at them, her eyes clear as day. "My wish is for you to help me plan my funeral."

"But Louise," Sarah pleaded.

"I want to plan it so that we can make it a grand party—something that celebrates my life and all the wonderful people in it," Louise said. "I don't want a sad one. My life has been wonderful, and it needs to be celebrated before I forget. Think of it as a party!"

Kate felt a breath catch in her chest. She forced her tears back and nodded. She looked at Sarah and then back at Louise. "Whatever you need," Kate said as she reached towards Louise's face and wiped the tears that fell from her best friend's eyes. "We've made our three wishes. Consider yours...granted."

The End

Bruce Lester's Letter

Dear Kate

Life is but fleeting. I know that for a fact.

Promise me that you will live your life. Go out each day and look up at the big sky. Take a deep breath in and let life fill you with love and wonder. Appreciate the blue skies, the green trees, the red, pink, and violet flowers; and remember how lucky you are to be alive.

Take Mr. Gibran's words and hold it in your heart. Let his words guide you as you live your life. "Life without liberty is like a body without spirit."

Let not tradition nor superstition, friend or foe, tie you down for you are you and you are free.

Love not with chains. Love not with fear. Love only with heart.

Thank you for being my friend.

Until we meet again,

Bruce

Helen and Philip's Conversation

Helen looked out the window as Philip drove her home. On one side of the road, trees lined the street behind a façade of small, quaint store fronts. On the other side, the dockside bustled with activity of shoppers, fishermen, families, and lovers. She kept her face turned away from Philip, lest he see her tears falling.

She couldn't believe that Kate had talked to her the way she did—in front of her friends, all strangers to Helen.

Her heart ached as she longed for the familiar touch of her late husband, Emilio.

Their marriage wasn't perfect, by no means. But he got her. He understood her like no one else in the world could. Emilio loved her and in her own way, she loved him too. It was both of them against the world.

When Emilio had first broached the subject of marriage to her, Helen wasn't interested. She believed she was destined for greater things, far beyond what he could ever give her. She had dreams of going to the United States; of forging a path of independence, away from her tyrannical parents. But she was nineteen and impetuous. At that time, the desire to free herself from the family chains was far greater than any dream. So she said yes.

Their marriage had been a good one—more for her than it was for Emilio, she was certain. Emilio gave her the keys to open every door—the freedom to do whatever she wanted. But when she fell pregnant just a few years later, everything changed. Once more, Helen had to set her dreams aside.

Kate had been a prickly baby. Colic took over their nights, and the infant cried to no end. With Emilio busy growing his business to support the family, Helen found herself alone with no one to talk to; no friends to turn to. They were all busy living active lives, while she'd married young. Kate...Kate was her retribution.

Postpartum depression hadn't been a *thing* back then. Depression was for the mentally insane, and those people were put into the 'basement'.

Hospitals masqueraded as bright white buildings of healthcare; but in the basement, the more sinister, misunderstood cases resided. Helen feared the basement, so instead, she wept in secret—quietly, behind closed doors, when the lights were out and no one was about.

It was a hard life, and Helen resented her daughter.

But as the years went by, she found in her daughter a companion. Kate looked up to her, and Helen enjoyed her daughter's admiration. Together, they became best friends.

Helen vowed to give her daughter the kind of mother she never had. The kind of mother who Kate could confide in. A mother who she could trust to tell her the truth and nothing but the truth.

And so, she did just that.

Helen didn't hold back. She gave Kate everything—her love, her friendship, her loyalty, and flagrant honesty.

And when Kate said she was leaving for the United States to follow the American, Helen's heart fell. Her daughter was leaving her.

She tried to warn Kate. She warned her that love was an illusion. She told her that the strawberries would rot and the champagne would distort her perception of reality.

For the first time in their mother and daughter relationship, Helen's words meant nothing.

Kate left. And Helen was left behind.

Kate followed her dreams—dreams that Helen herself had once held close to her heart. She should have been happy for her daughter. That's what a good mother would have done. Instead, anger and betrayal filled her heart, burning it from within.

And when Emilio died—when he took his life—Helen saw it as yet another betrayal. Yet again, she'd been abandoned.

"Helen?" Philip's voice cut through her thoughts. "Are you okay?"

Helen sniffed and nodded. Discreetly, she used her fingers to wipe her tears.

"Is there anything you want to talk about?" Philip asked.

Philip was a priest, and priests were God's messengers. Helen needed to unburden. No one else but the doctor and perhaps the undertaker knew that Emilio had committed the greatest sin of all; that he had taken his own life. She feared for his soul; for his eternal damnation. Helen feared that she would never again be reunited with her one true love. "My husband didn't die of a heart attack," she said softly.

Philip didn't say anything and kept his eyes on the road.

"He took his own life," Helen continued. "And I'm afraid that God will never forgive him." Tears fell from her eyes. Her heart opened up and sobs of worry, regret, anger, and love escaped from her throat.

Helen poured her heart out to Philip in the hope that through him, God was listening. She talked until there was nothing more to say. She cried until there were no more tears to shed. She wept until she was overcome with exhaustion.

Philip pulled into a carpark by the dockside, facing the water. "Helen," he said, "Neither death nor life, nor angels nor rulers, nor things present nor things to come, nor powers, nor height nor depth, nor anything else in all creation, will be able to separate us from the love of God in Christ Jesus our Lord."

Helen wiped her tears, sniffling at every breath. Her hands trembled on her lap.

"God sees everything," Philip said. "And he knows everything. He knows you are grieving, and he grieves alongside you."

She turned to face Philip. His face had a kindness that she felt she was not deserving of. "It's my fault he ended his life. I was terrible to him." Helen covered her face, her shoulders shaking violently. "I didn't even get to tell him how much I loved him."

"People make their own choices, and we are not responsible for the choices they make. You loved your husband as he loved you."

"But I never got the chance to tell him." Helen was weary.

"God hears us, Helen. He hears everything in your heart and he knows the pain you are in. Lift it all up the Lord and live in the Spirit of God. Forgive yourself, for God has already forgiven you."

For I am sure that neither death nor life, nor angels nor rulers, nor things present nor things to come, nor powers, nor height nor depth, nor anything else in all creation, will be able to separate us from the love of God in Christ Jesus our Lord.
~Romans 8:31-39

NEXT IN THE MULBERRY LANE SERIES: In Three Years

Find out what happens next for Sarah, Kate, and Louise in Book 3 of the Mulberry Lane series, In Three Years.

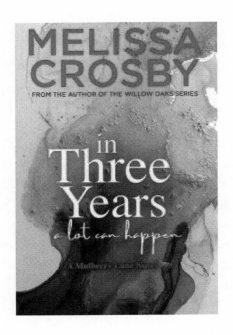

A Letter to You

Dear Friends

Thank you for choosing to read *Three Wishes - A Mulberry Lane Novel, Book 2.*

When I first began writing the Mulberry Lane series, I knew I wanted to write a story that would convey just how extraordinary women are. In the last book, I explored the issues and hidden burdens that many women carry as daughters, sisters, mothers, wives, and partners.

In this sequel to Tea for Three, you will find a strong focus on mother-and-daughter relationships; particularly the one between Kate and her mom. We follow Kate, who is originally from the Philippines, as she struggles to navigate her new life in the United States; whilst still trying to fulfill her obligations as a dutiful daughter as dictated by her deep-seated cultural and familial traditions.

While Louise's relationship with her stepdaughter Abby has gone from strength to strength, she still carries a heavy cross for her daughter, Madison, with whom she is estranged.

And just as Sarah comes out the other side of grief, following the death of her husband; one of her children is diagnosed with a disorder that proves too much for Sarah to bear.

Once again, Kate, Louise, and Sarah find themselves in the face of misfortune and adversity of which they are powerless to change. But as they have already once proven to us, the bonds of their friendship and their faith in God are much stronger than anything that life can throw at them.

I hope you enjoy your visit to Carlton Bay, and I look forward to catching up with you in the next book, *In Three Years*.

Hearing from my readers is one of the things I most enjoy about being an author. You can contact me through my website at www.melissacrosby.com

Kind wishes

Melissa Crosby

READ OTHER BOOKS BY MELISSA CROSBY:
Willow Oaks Series - Sweet Romance

- Book 1: Love Me True
- Book 2: Love Me Maybe
- Book 3: Love Me Again
- Book 4: Love Me Always
- Book 5: Love Me Timeless

Mulberry Lane Series - Inspirational Women's Fiction

- Book 1: Tea for Three
- Book 2: Three Wishes
- Book 3: In Three Years

Collections:

- A Willow Oaks Sweet Romance Collection: Volume 1 - Books 1-3
- A Willow Oaks Sweet Romance Collection: Volume 2 - Books 4-6

About the Author

Melissa Crosby lives in Wellington, New Zealand with her husband, two children, and their adopted rescue pets, Evie and Zuko. She enjoys writing inspirational women's fiction and heartwarming small town romance.

To be the first to get updates on new releases and freebies, sign up to her newsletter at www.melissacrosby.com.

Read more at https://melissacrosby.com/.

Made in the USA
Middletown, DE
19 April 2021

37937803R00170